I0423399

Adult Coloring Book

100 Patterns For Stress Relief

Jay Martin

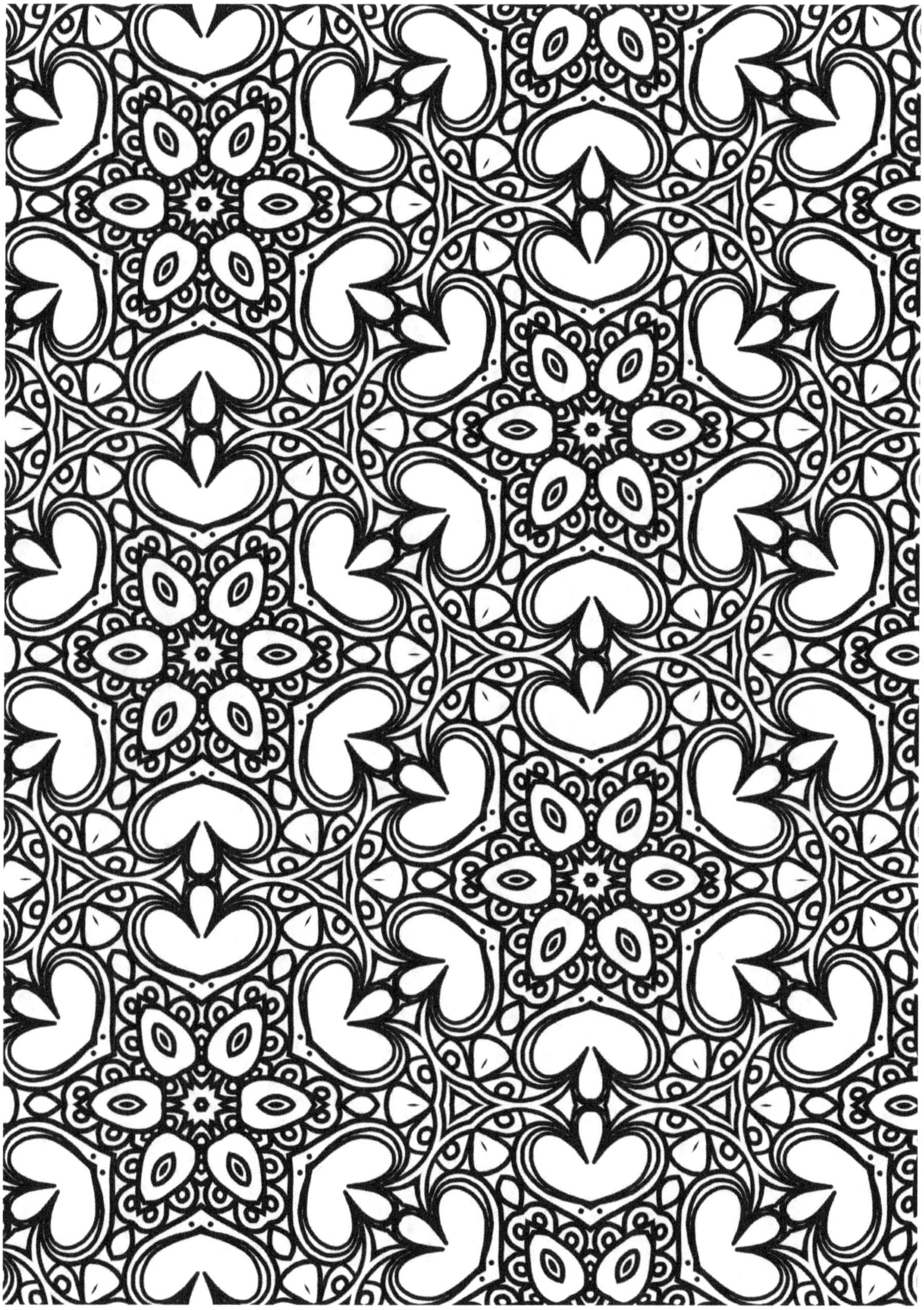

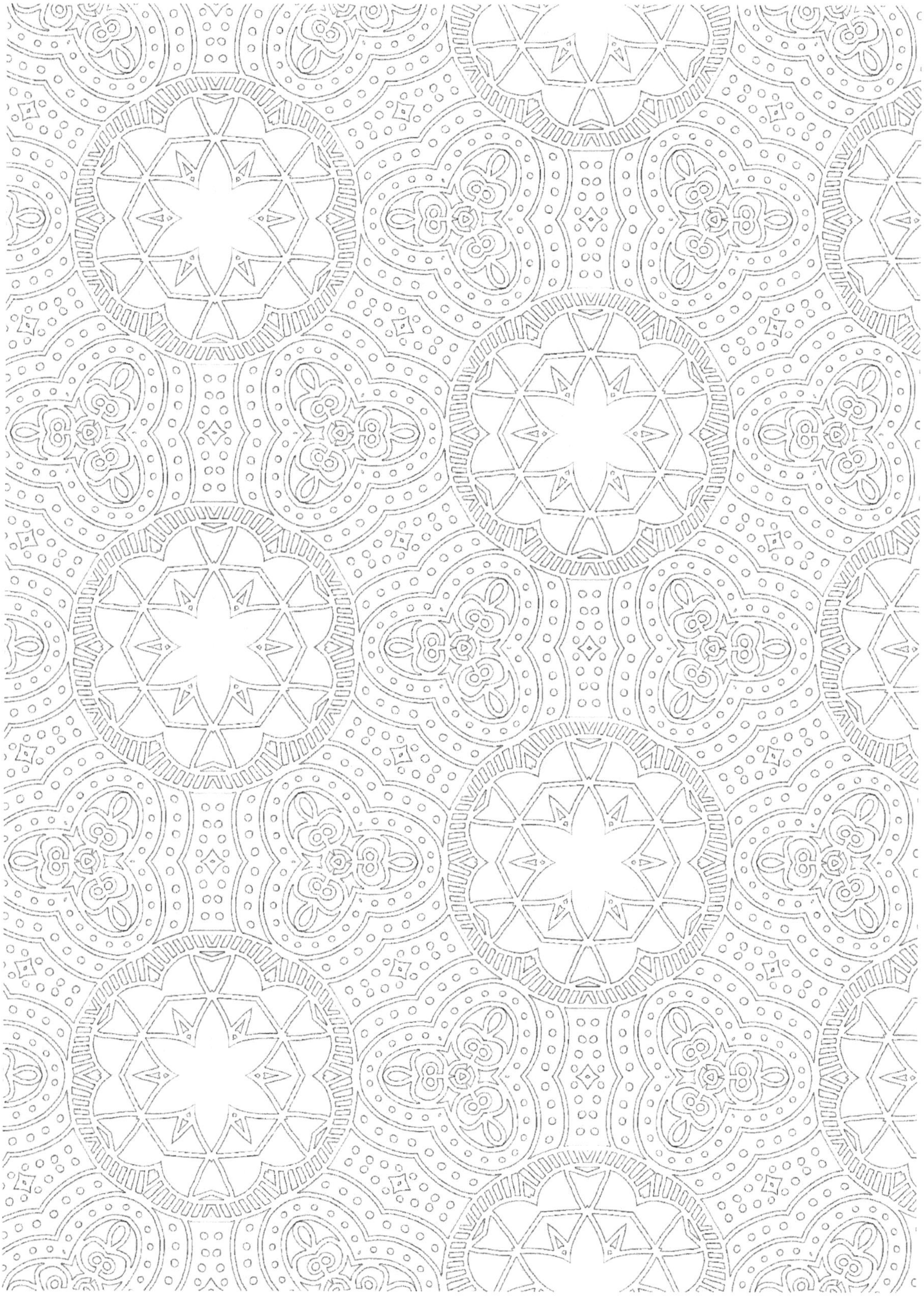

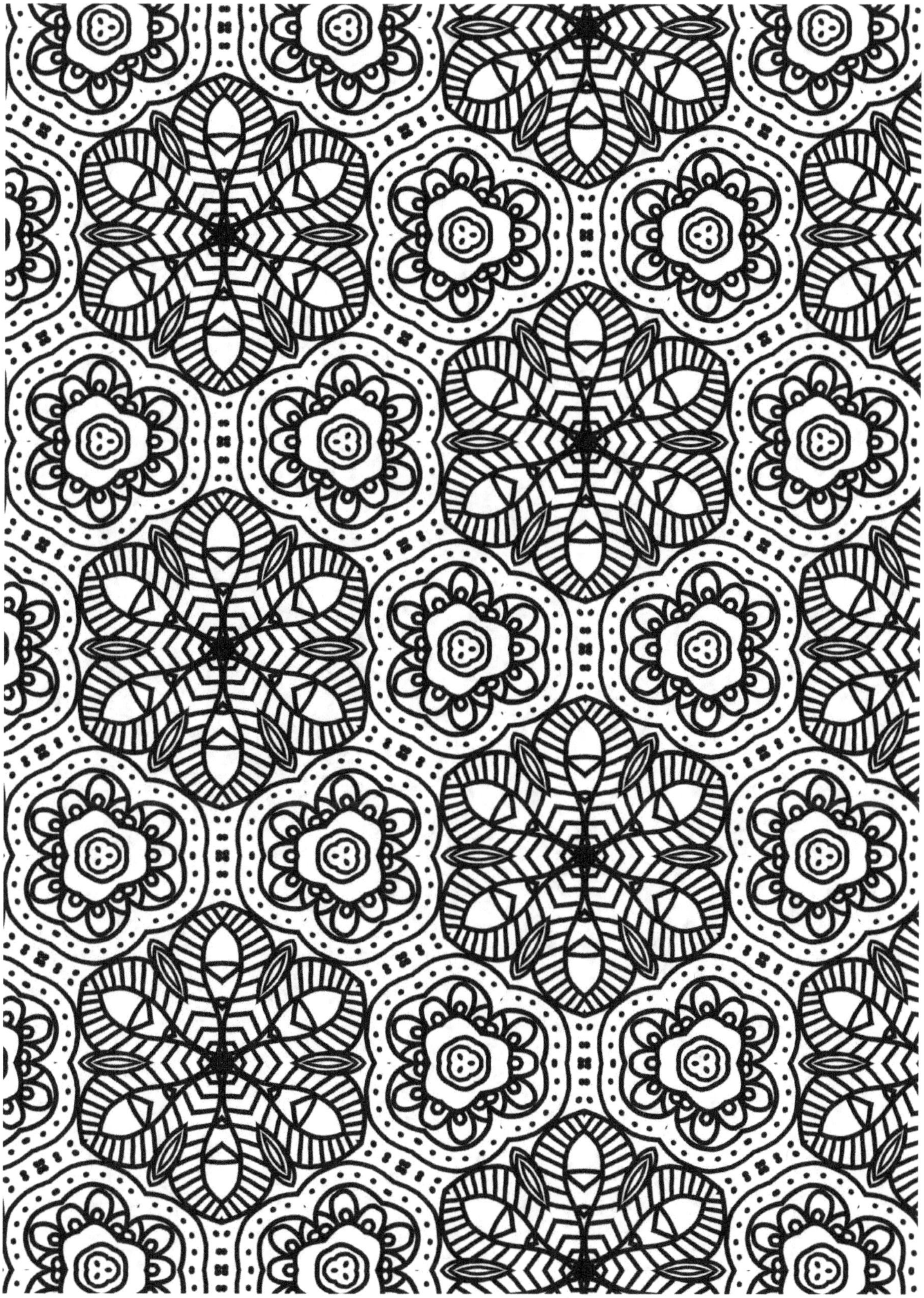

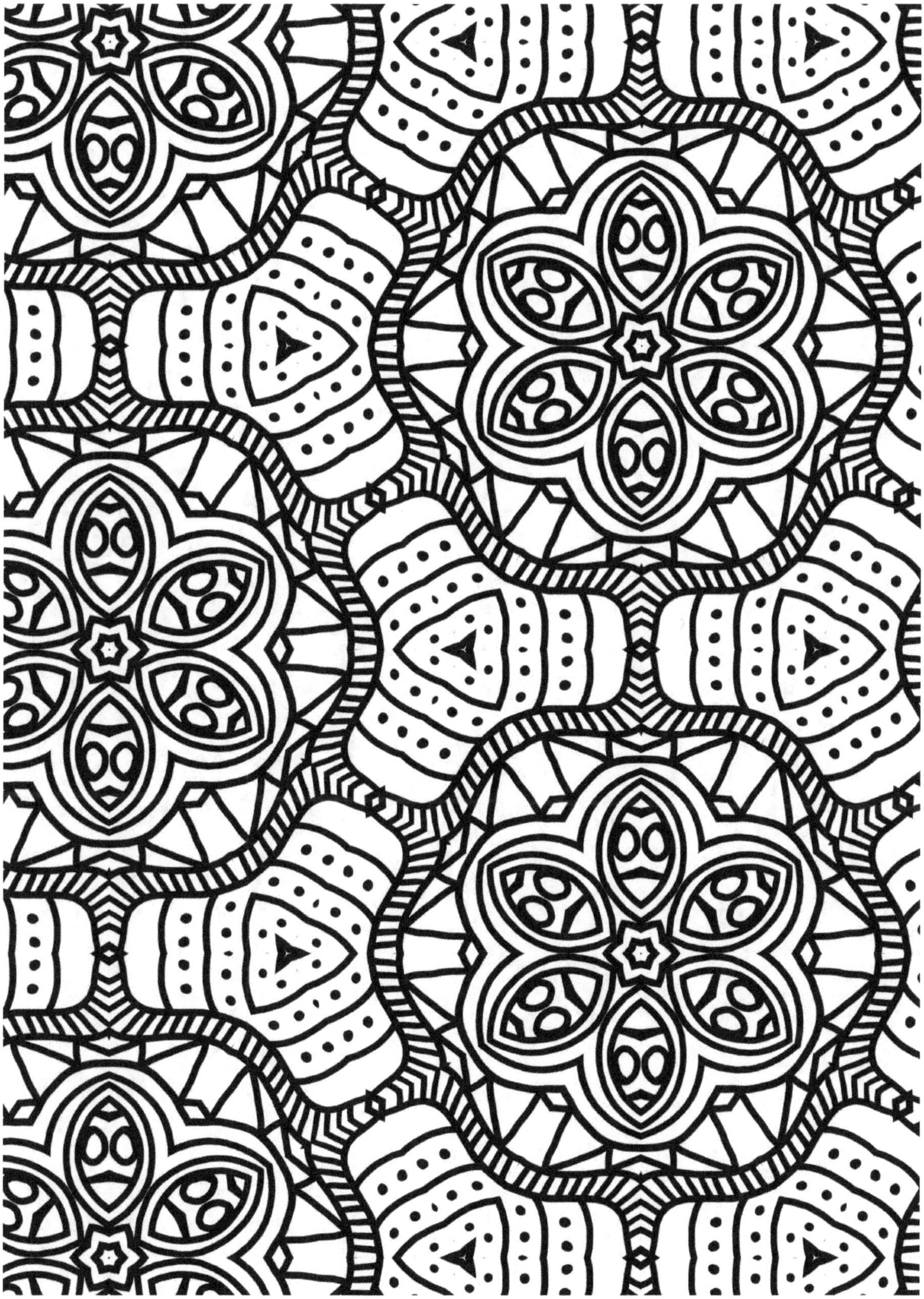

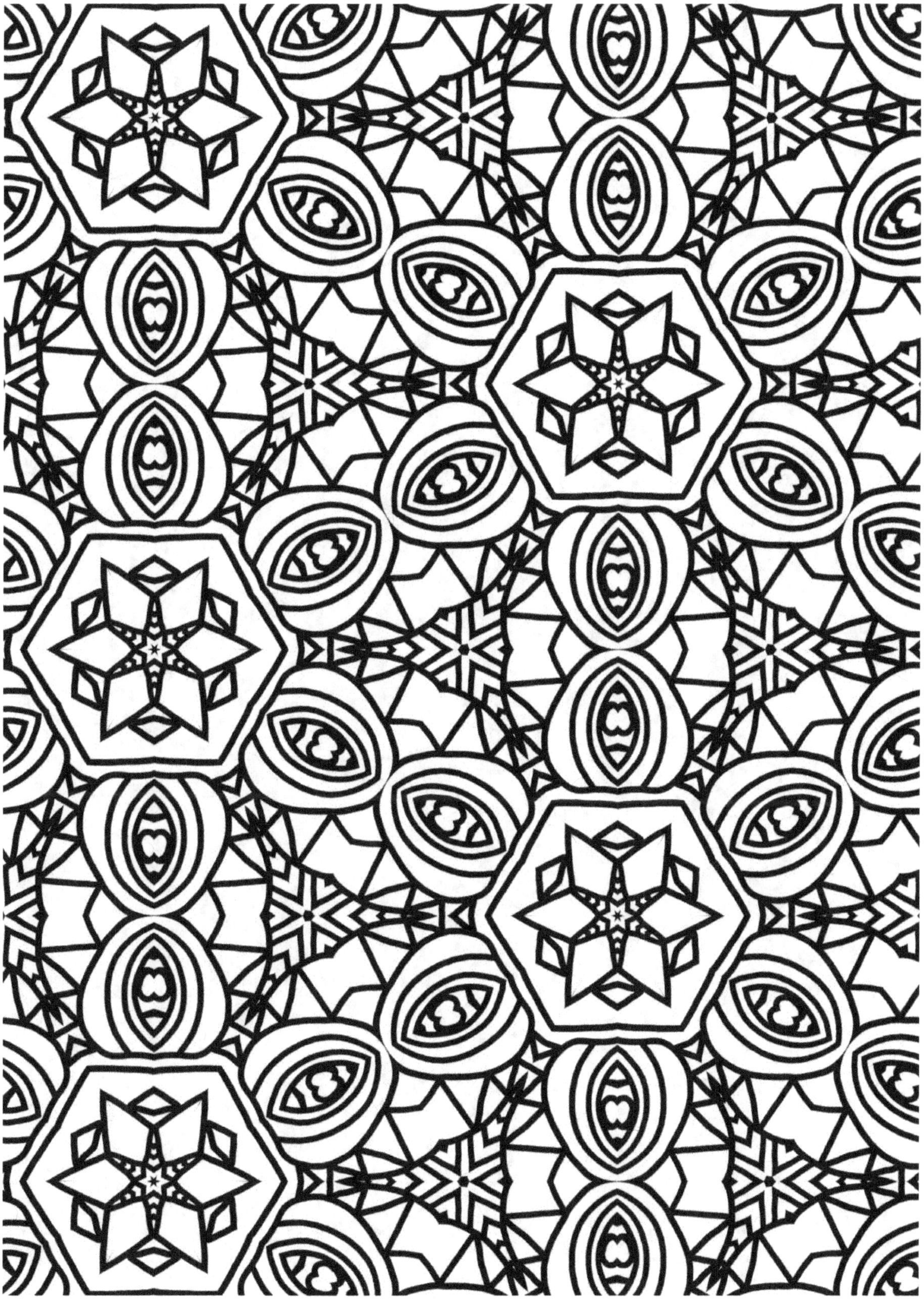

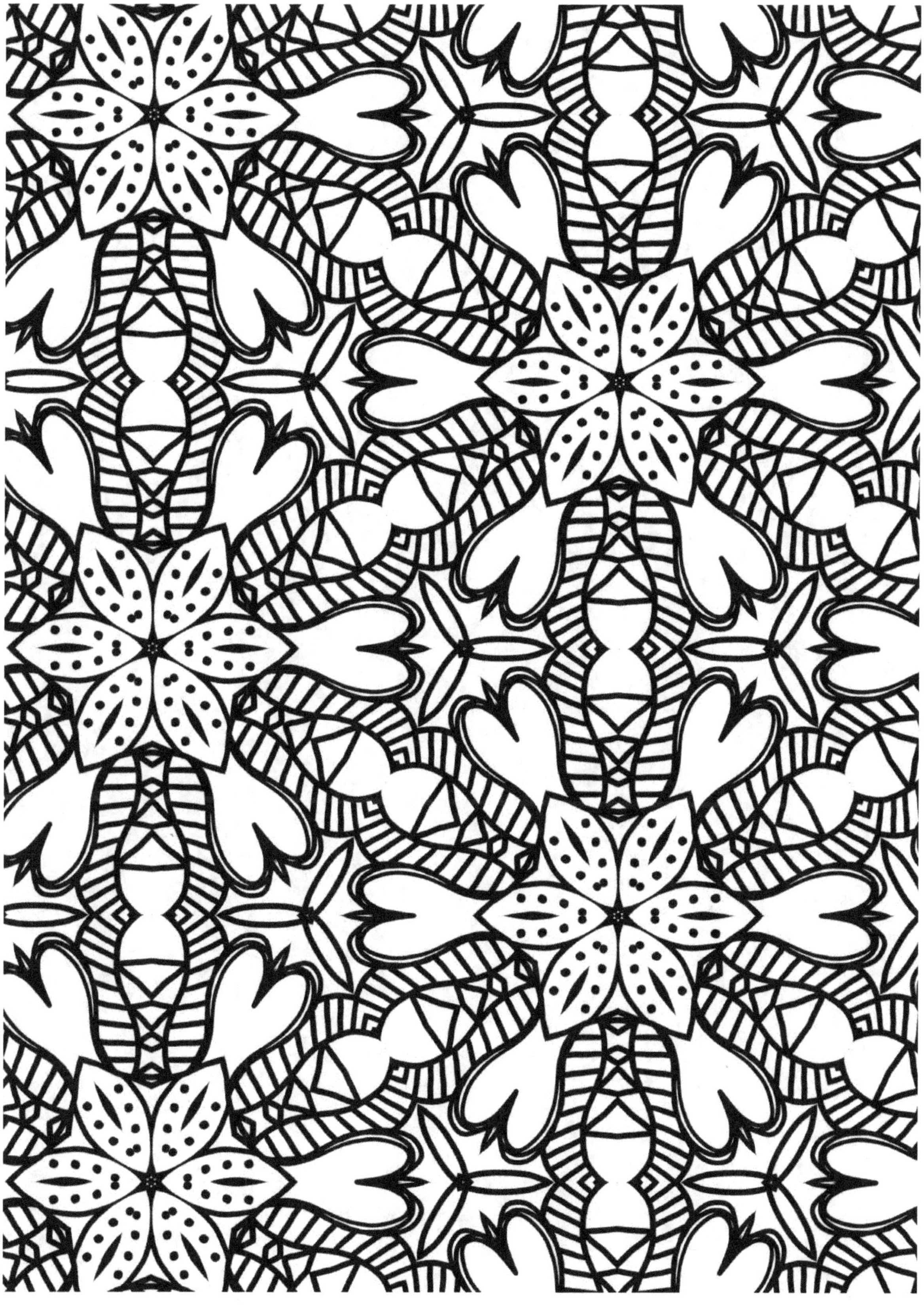

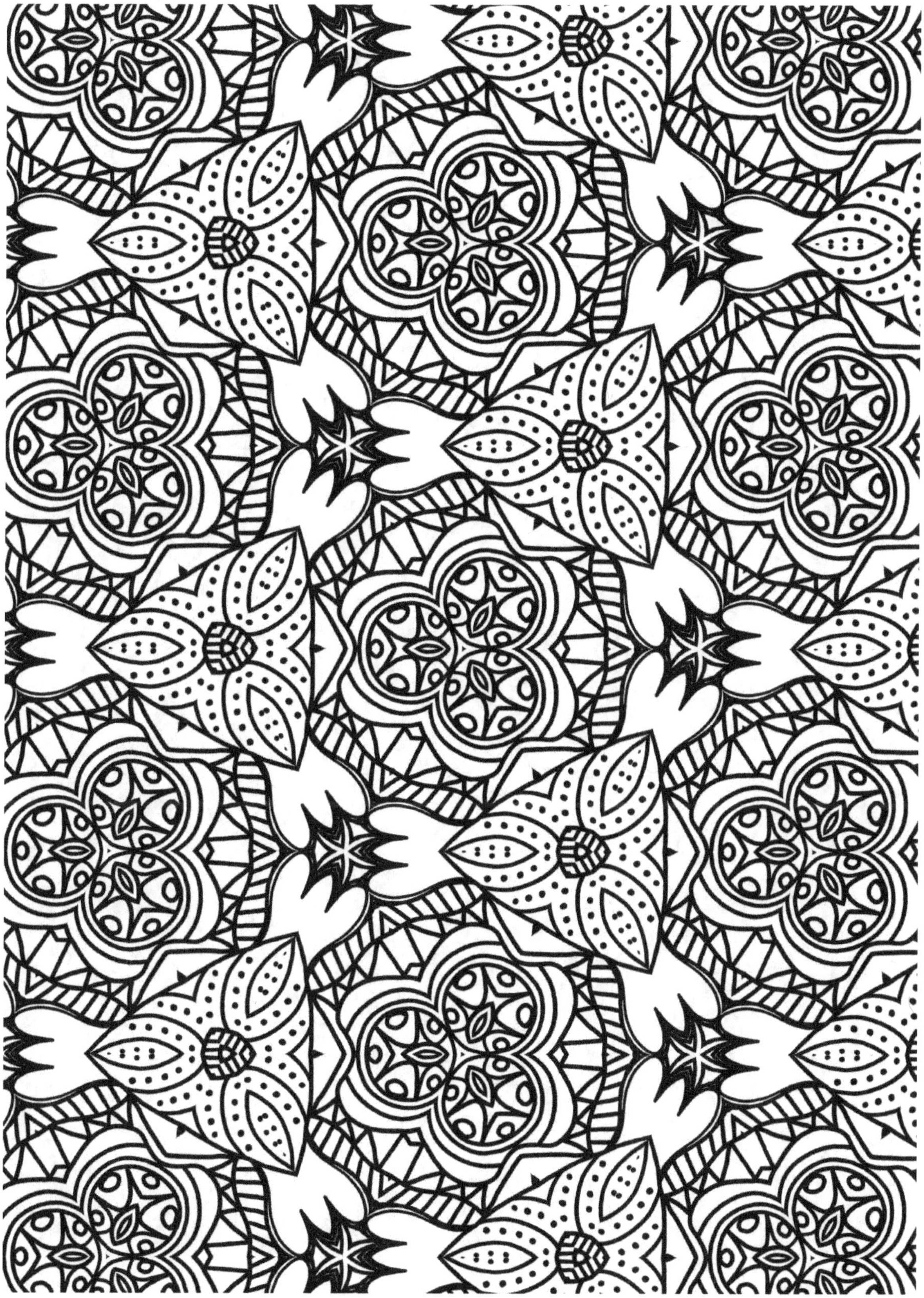

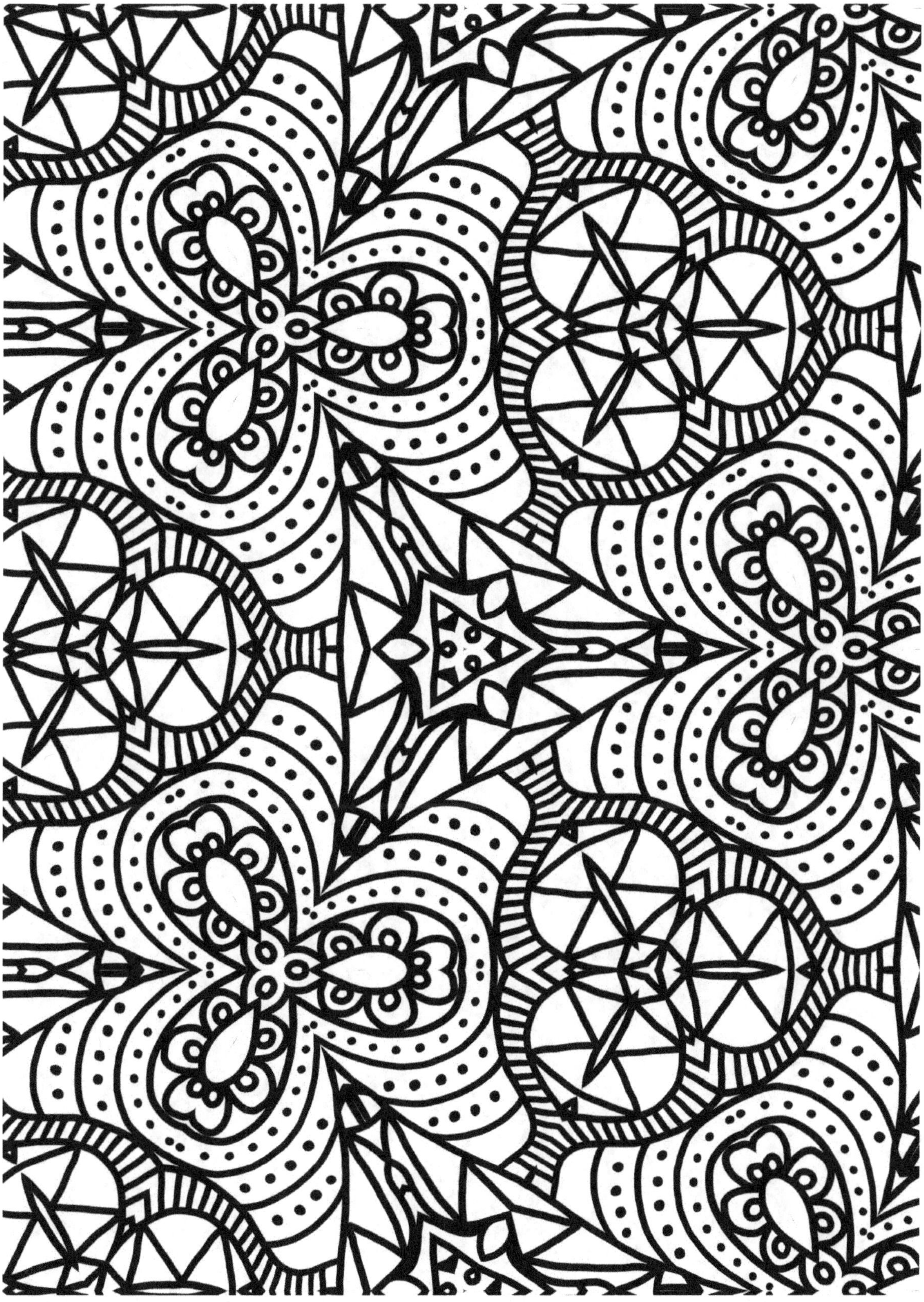

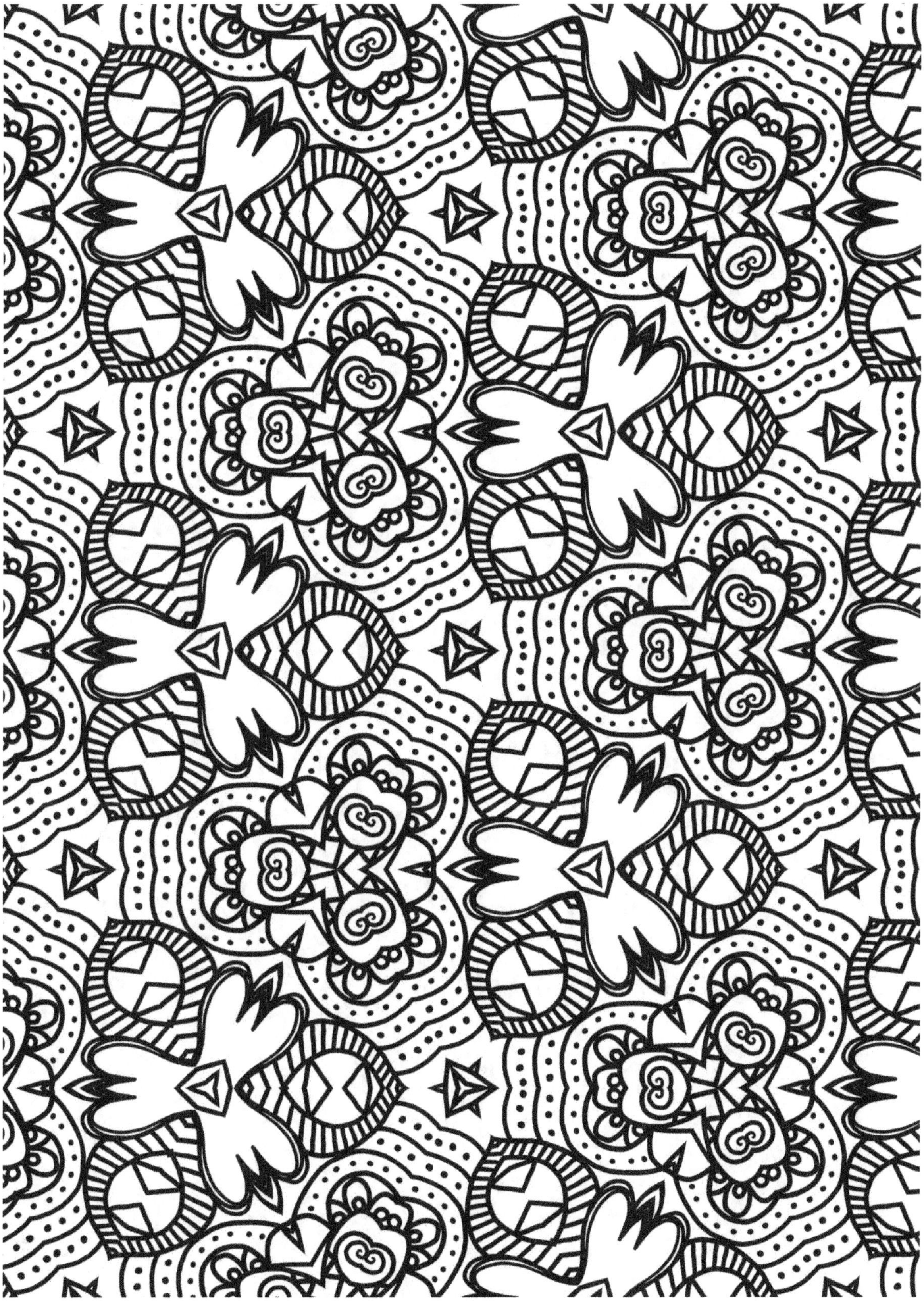

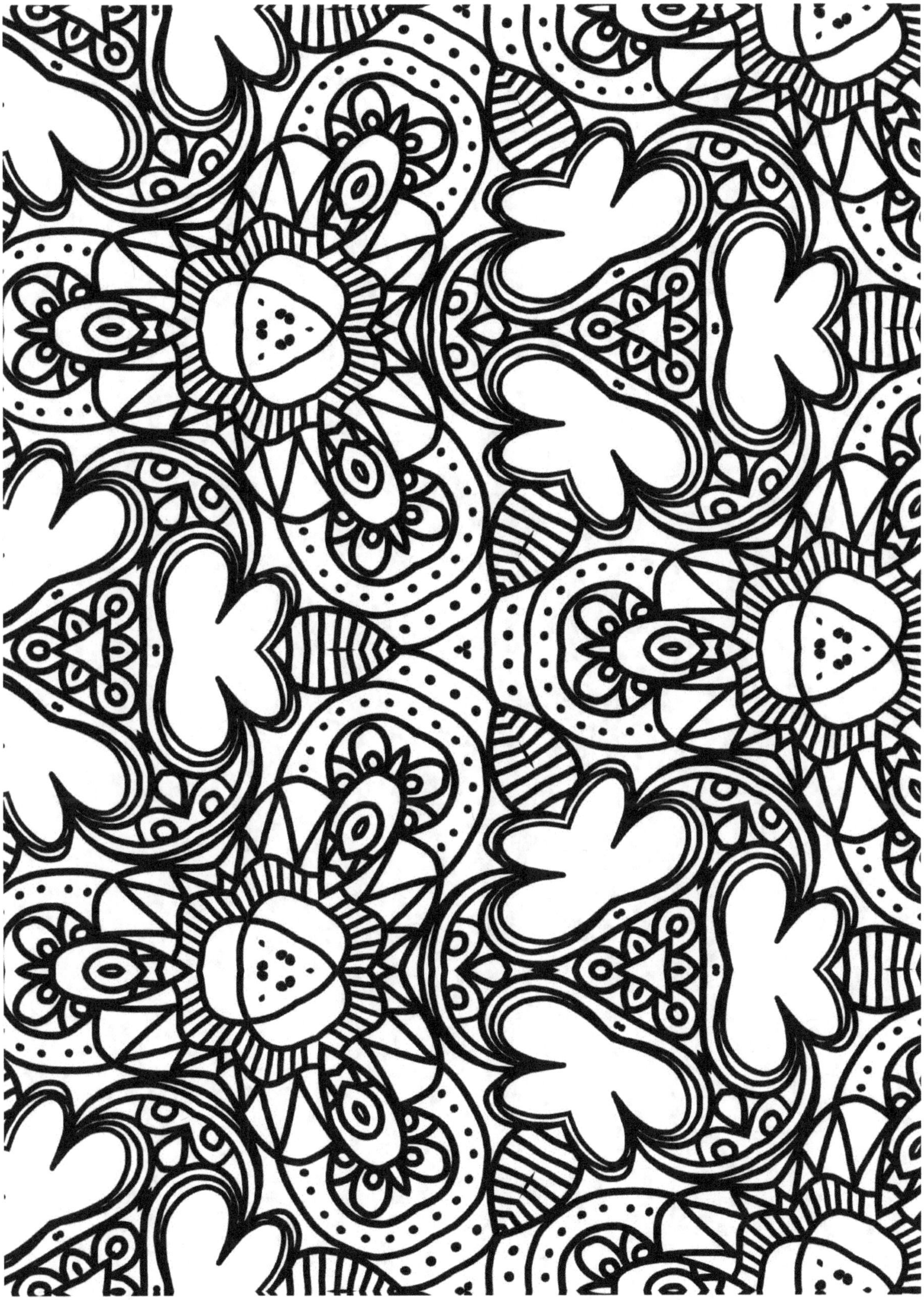

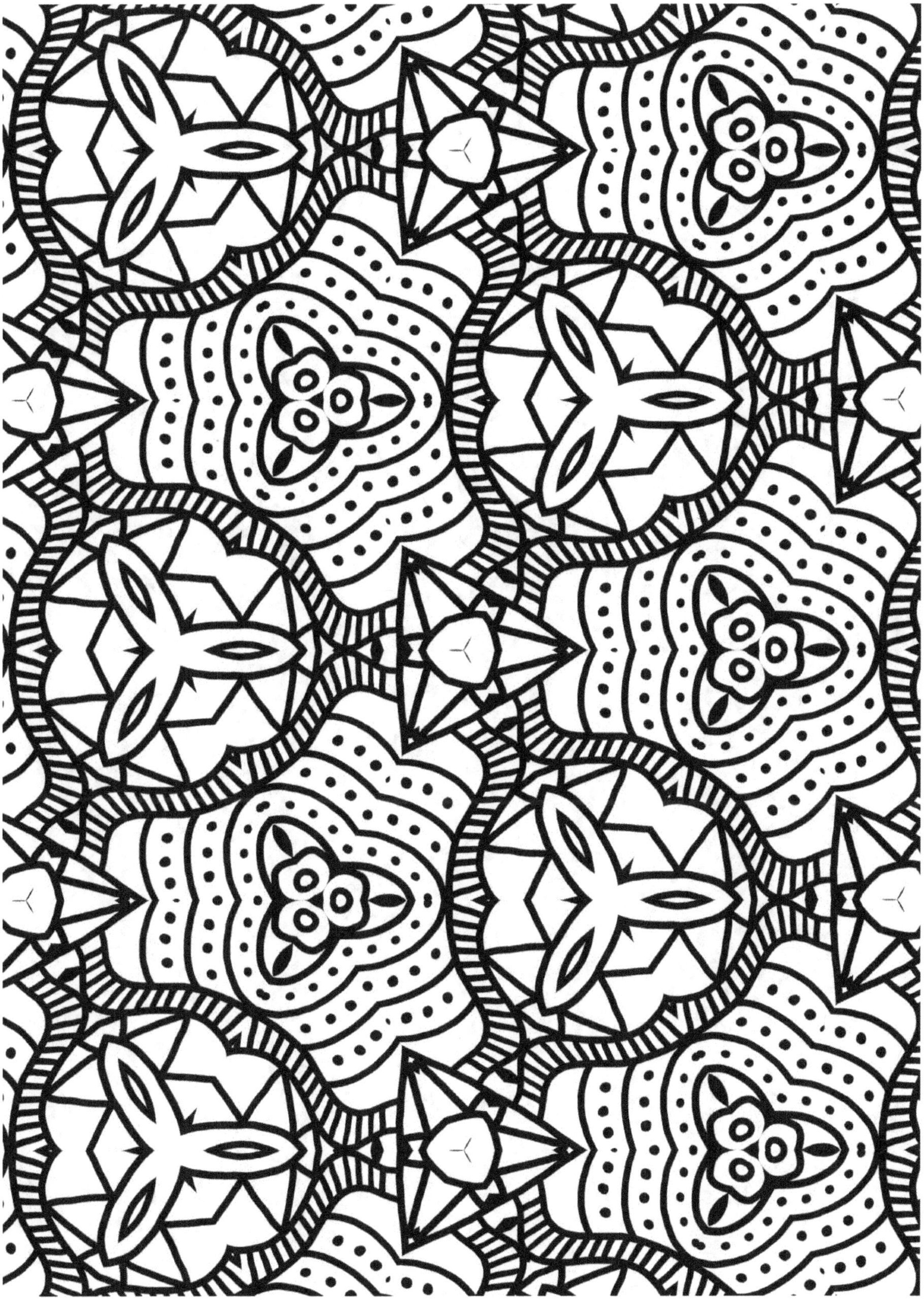

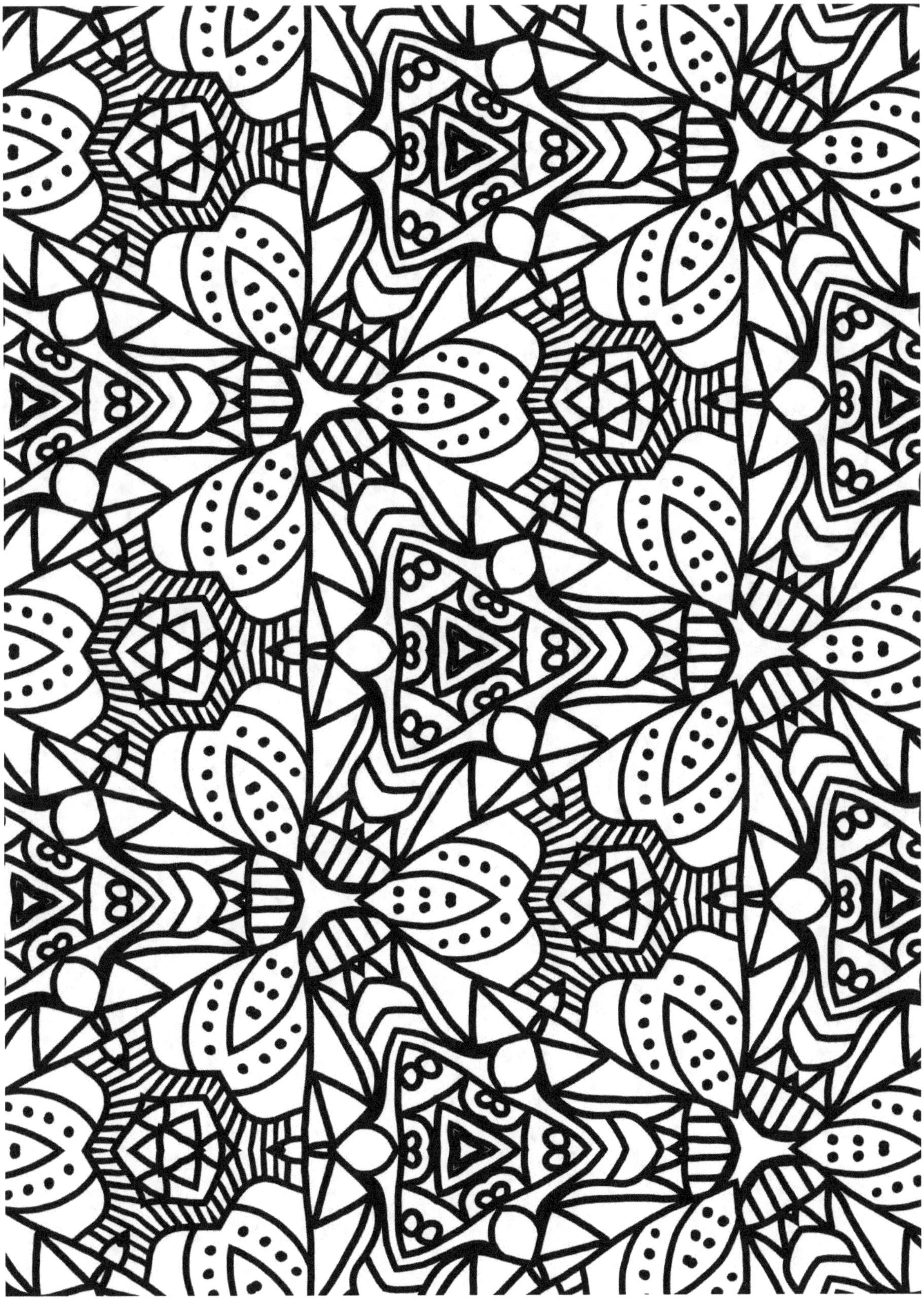

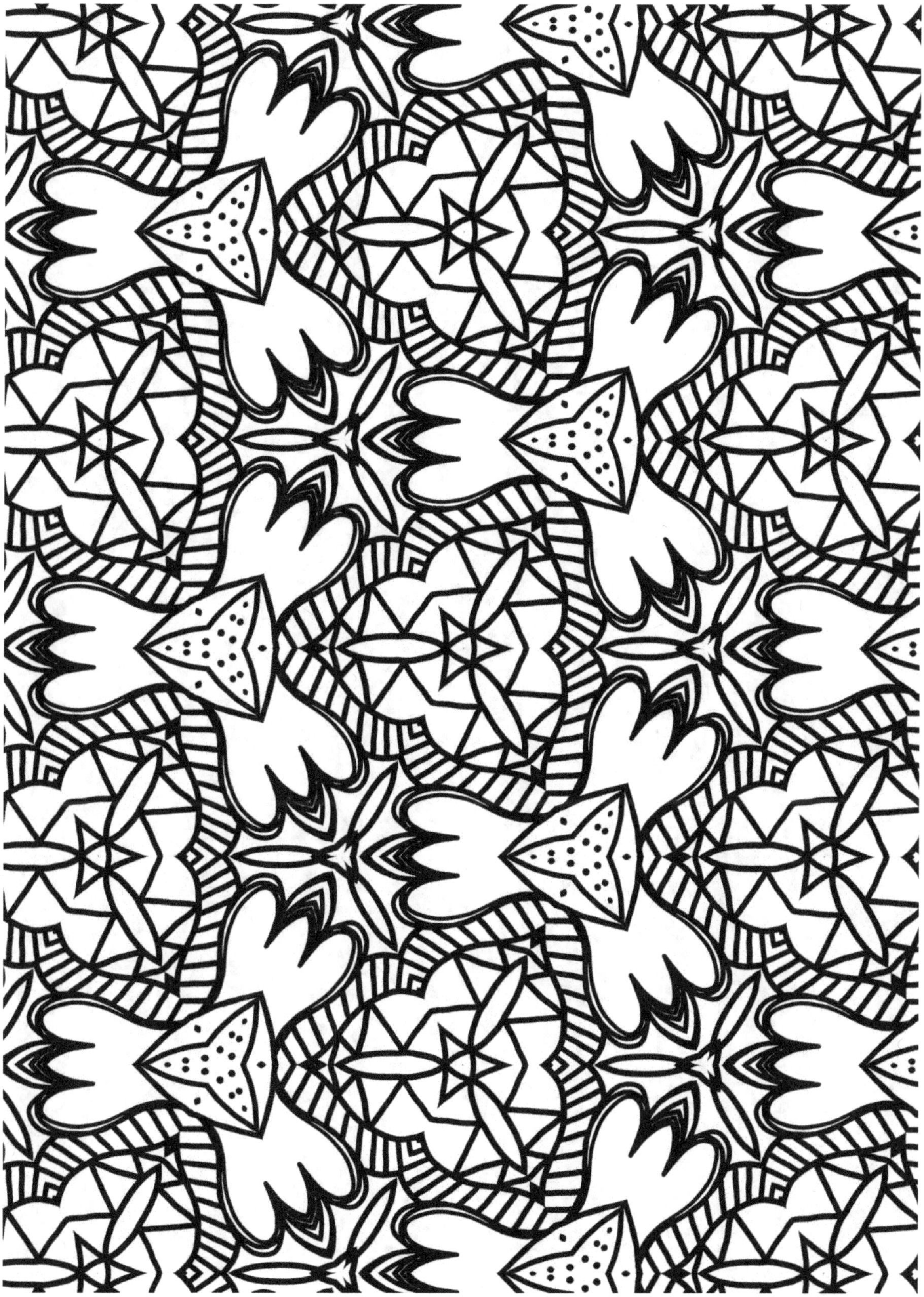

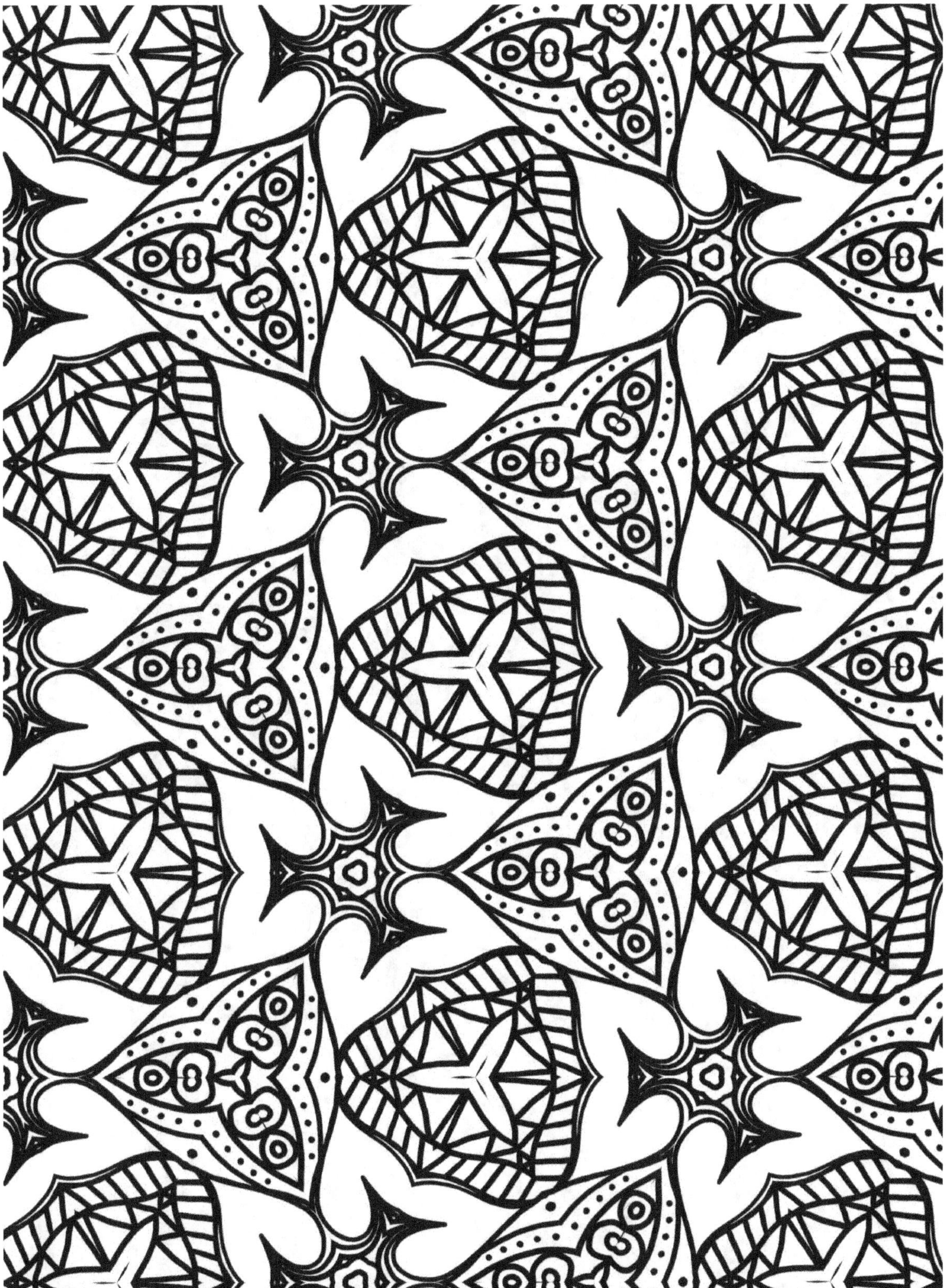

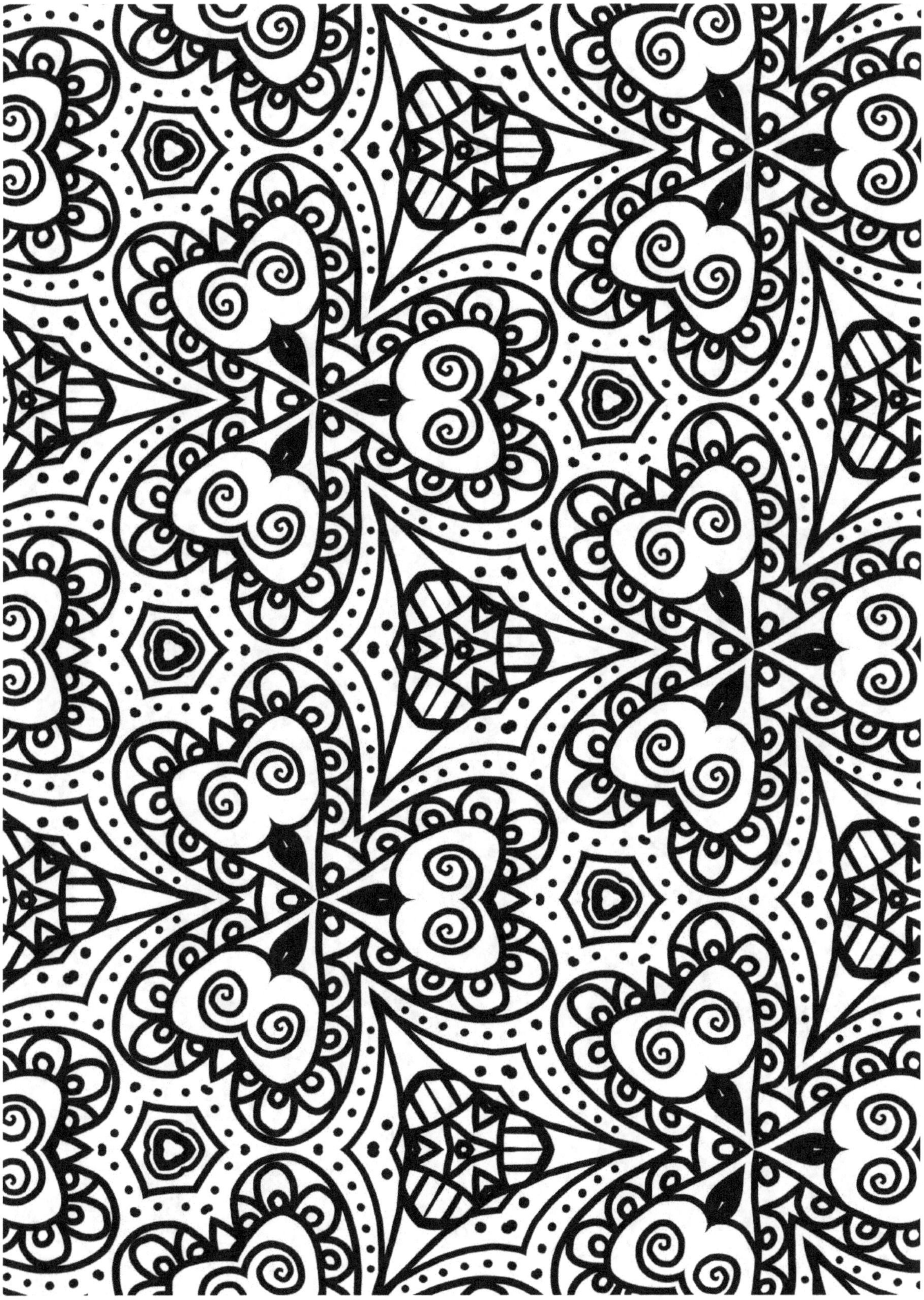

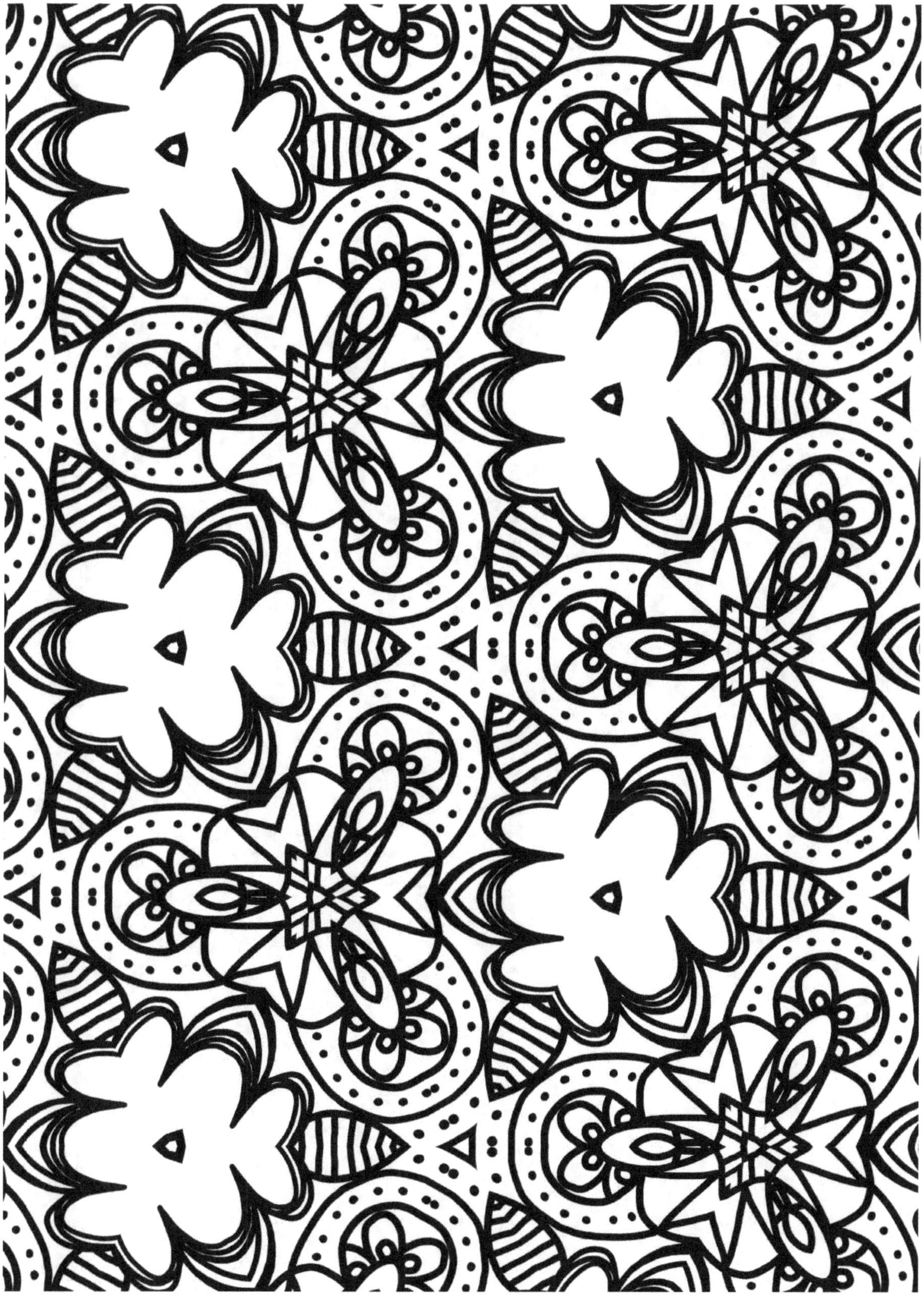

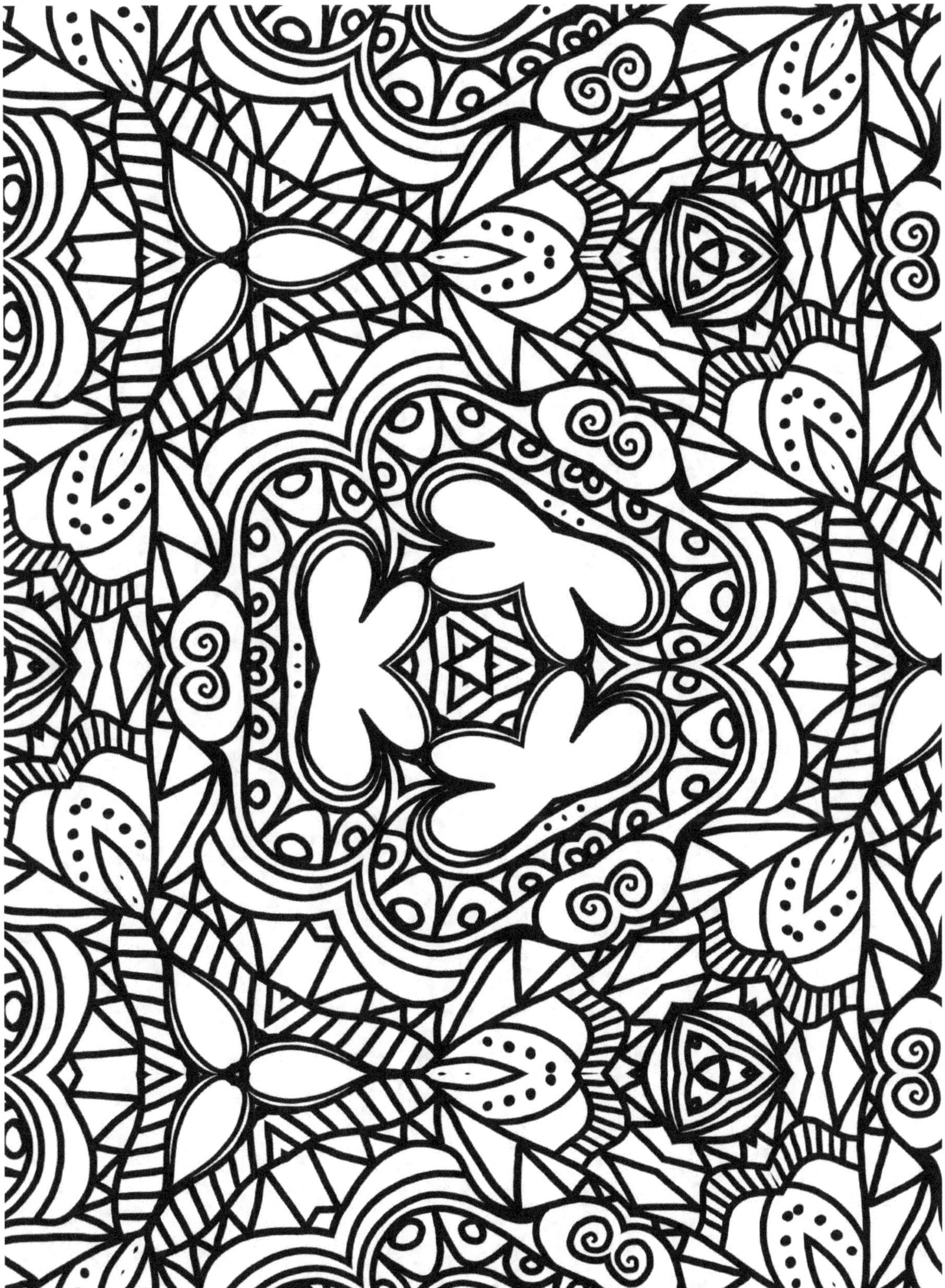

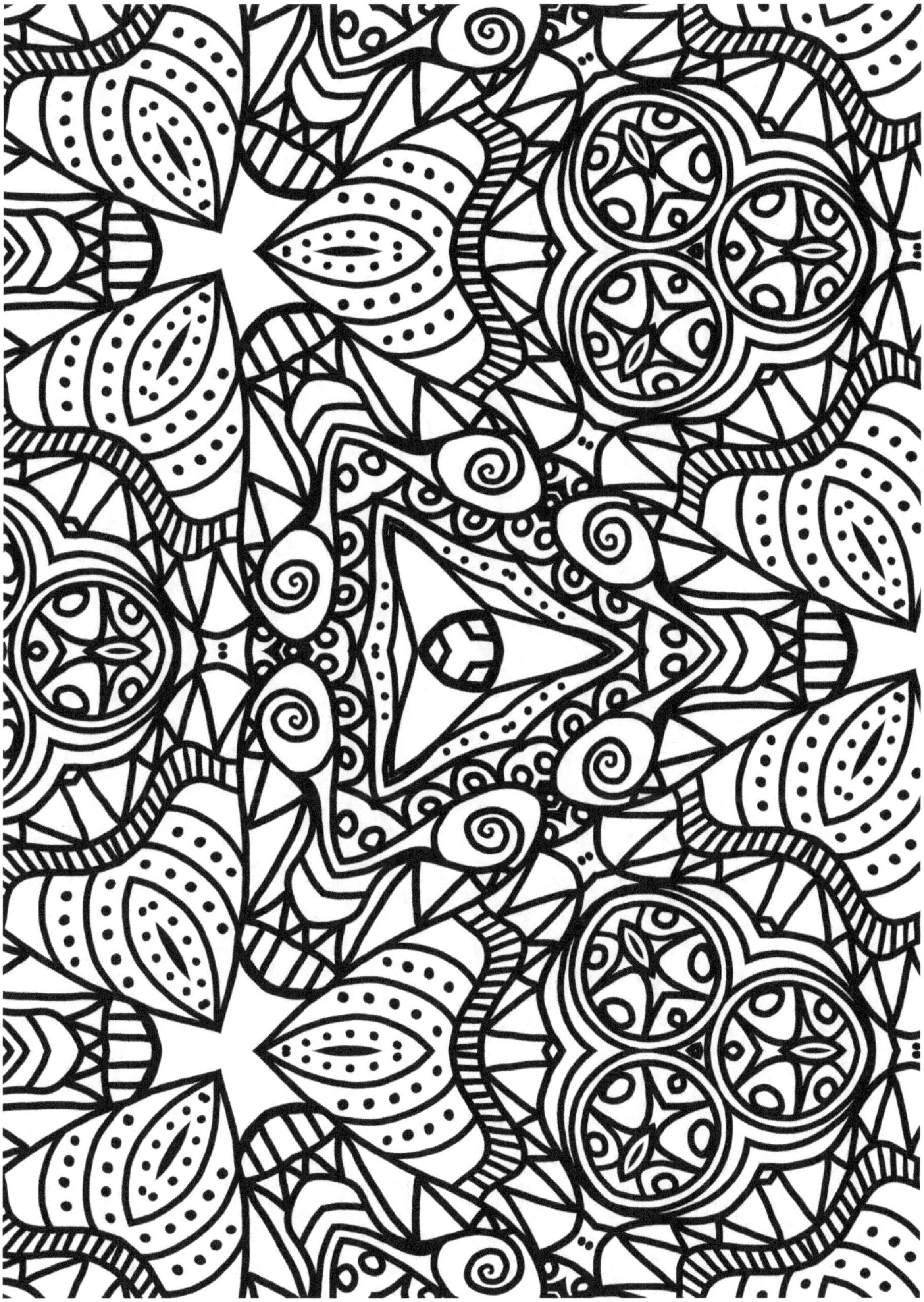

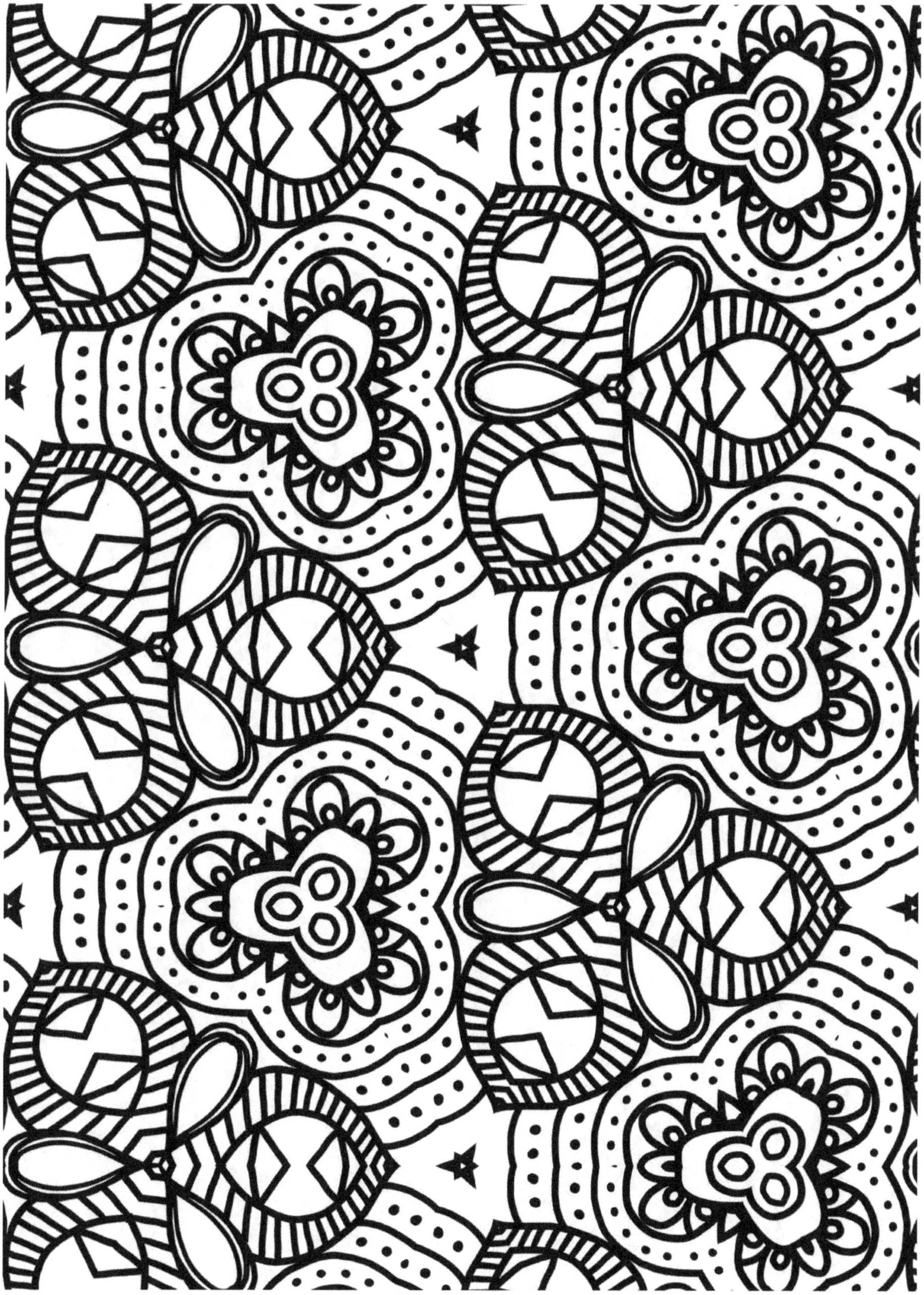

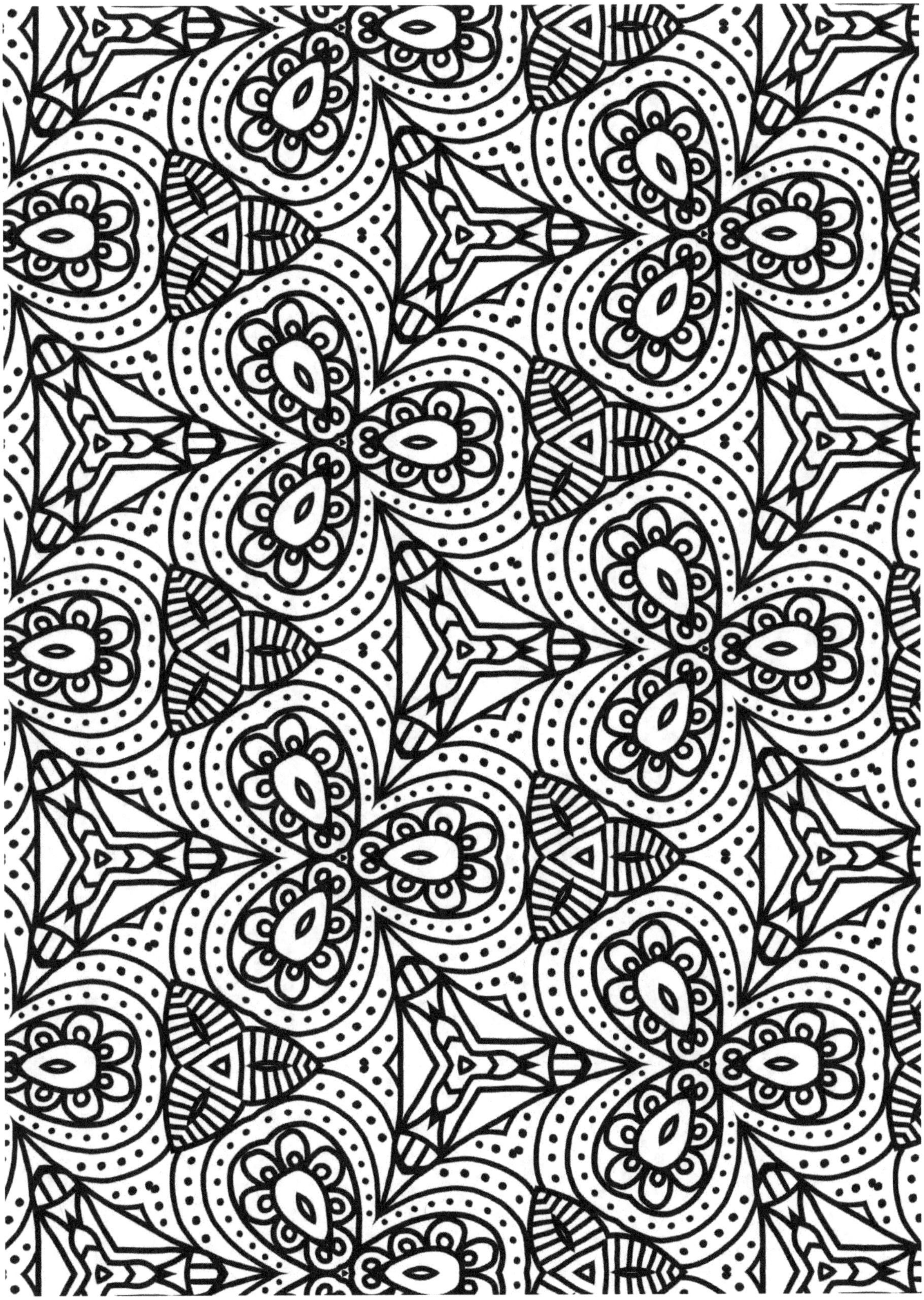

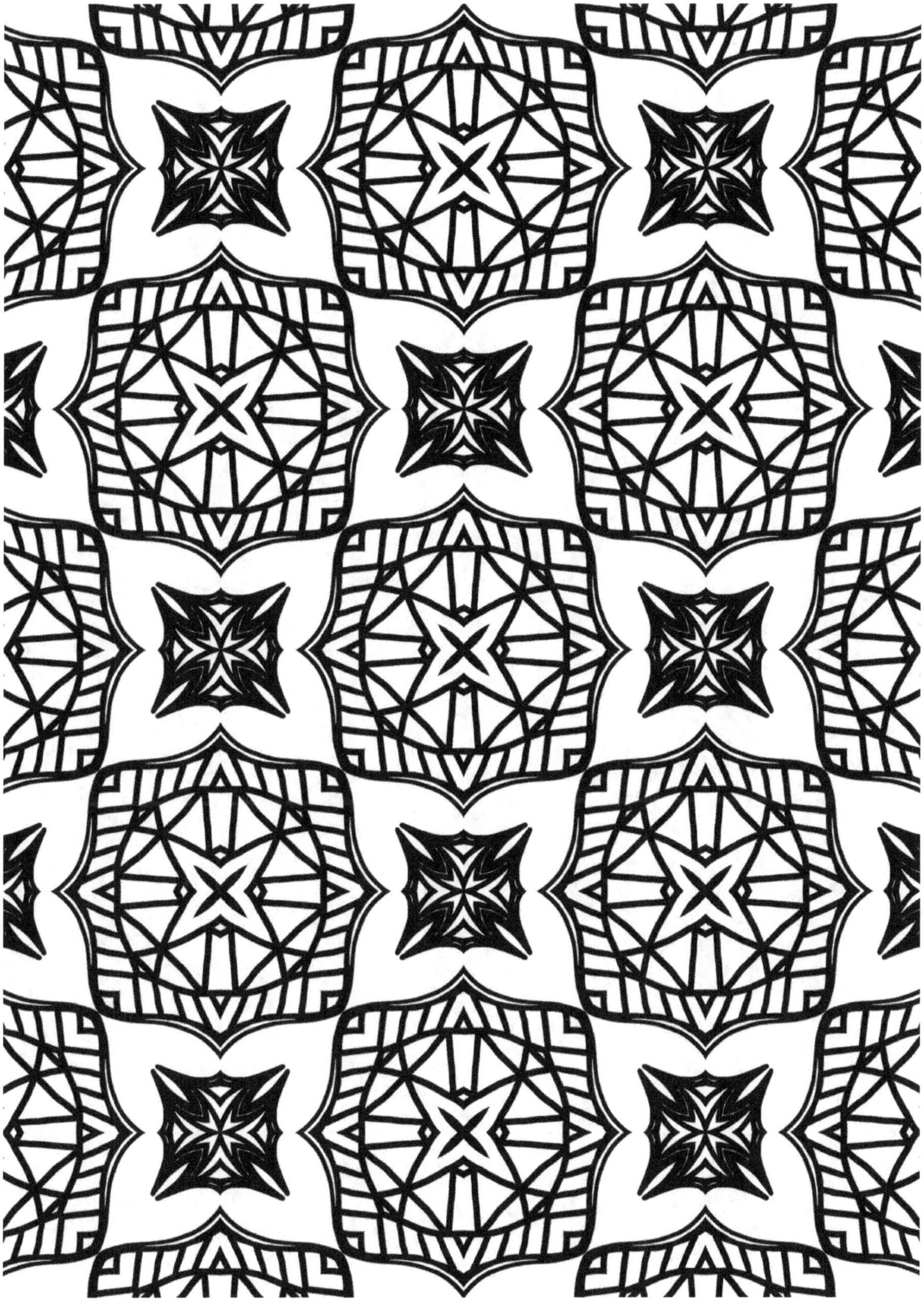

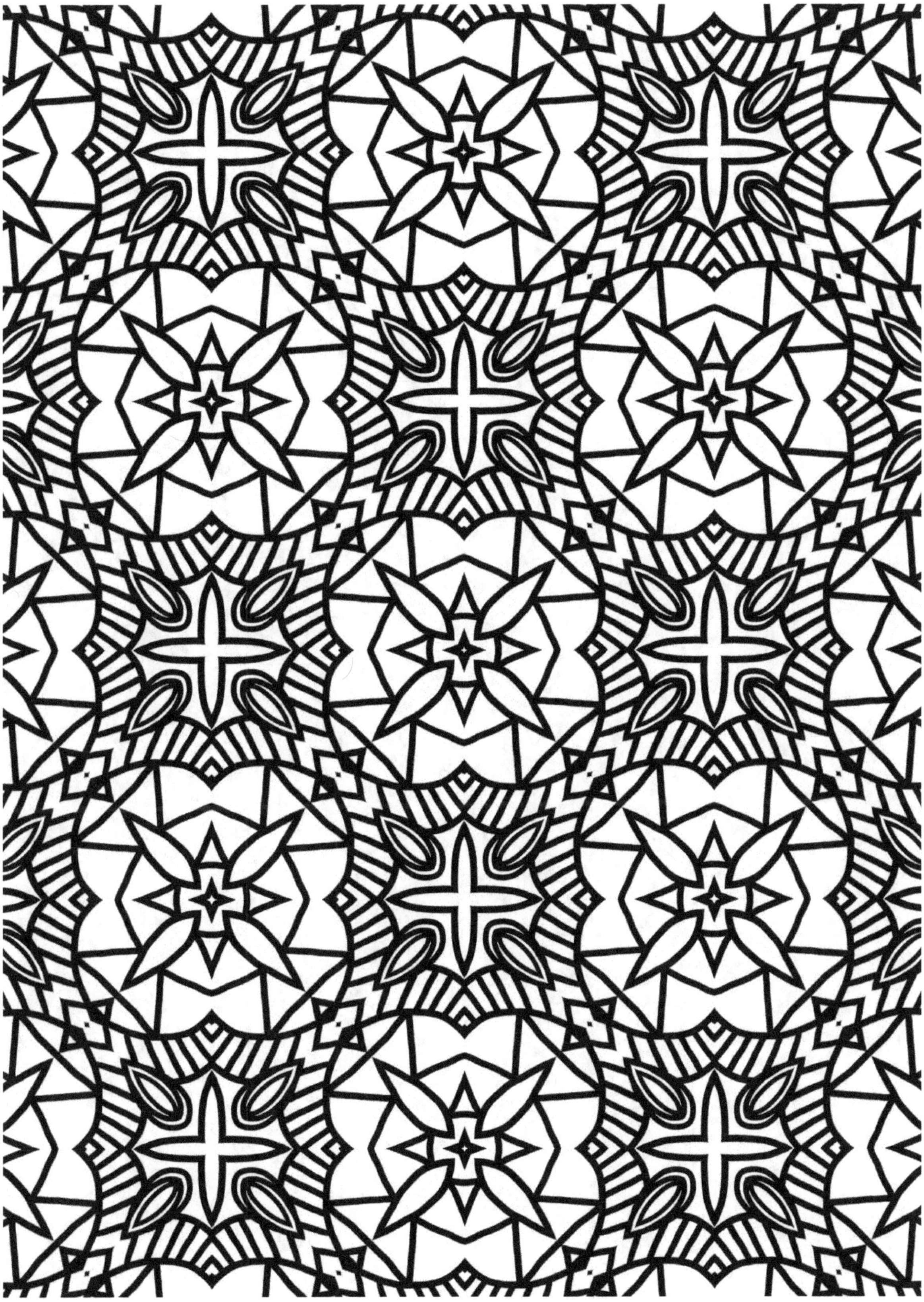

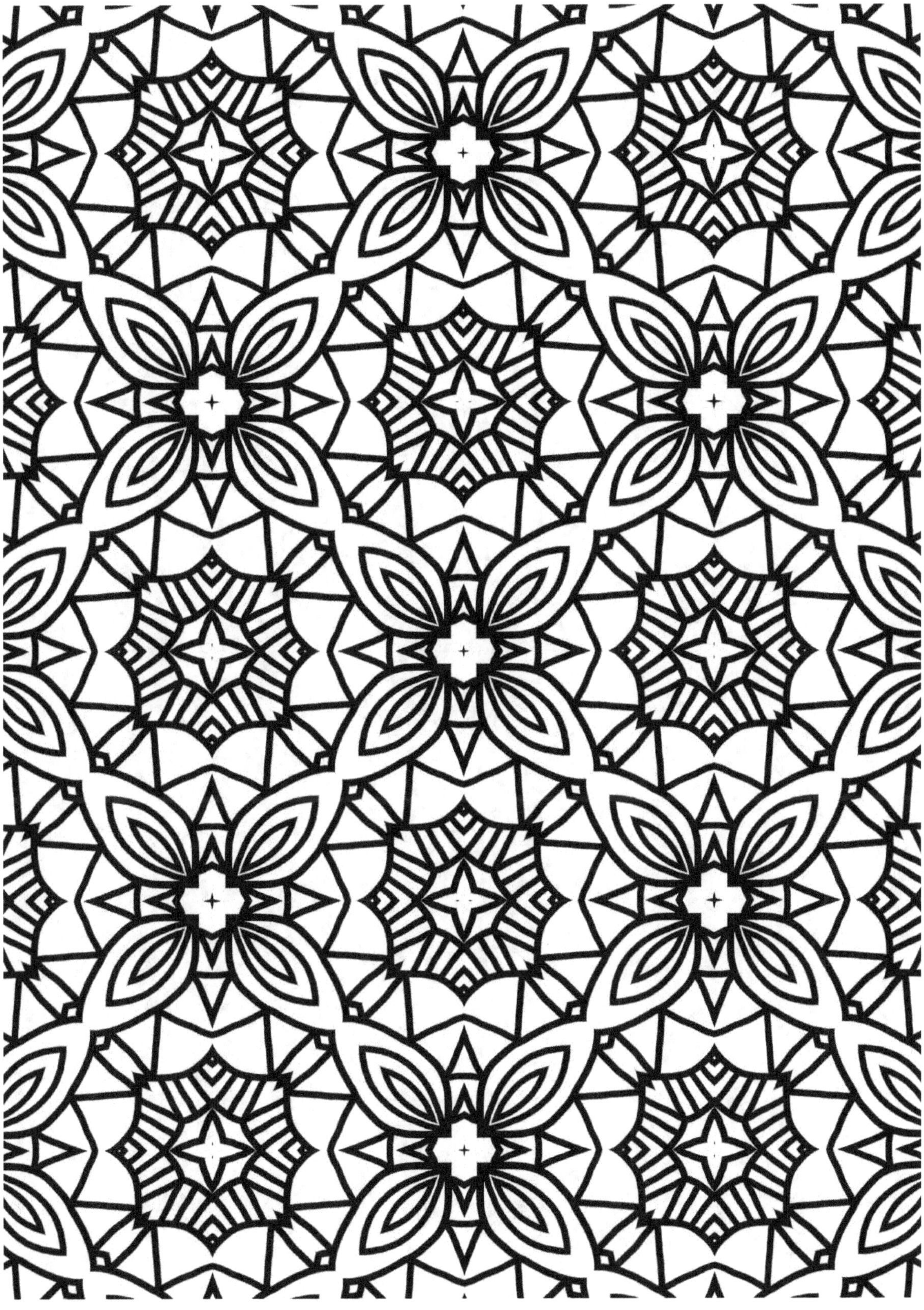

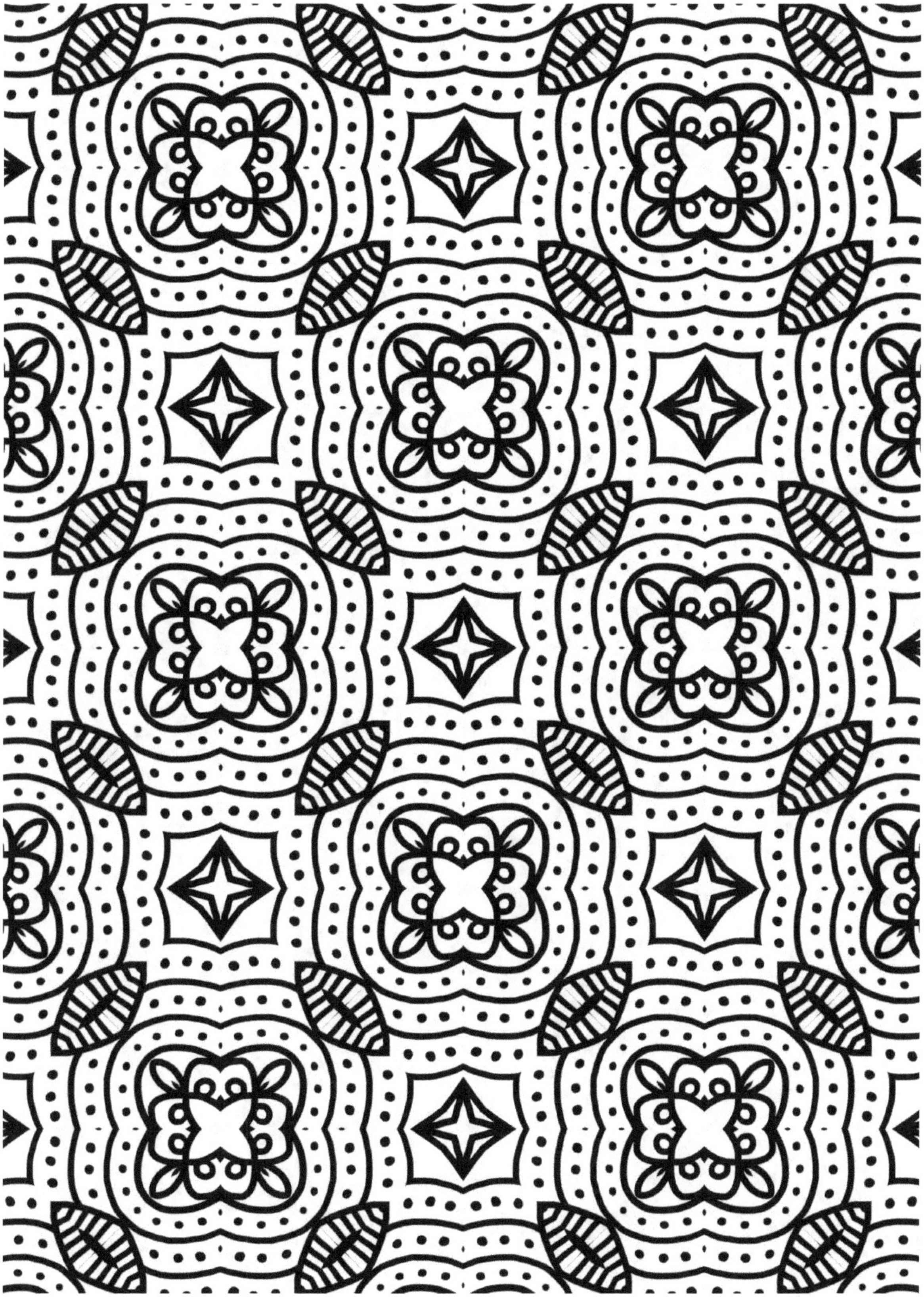

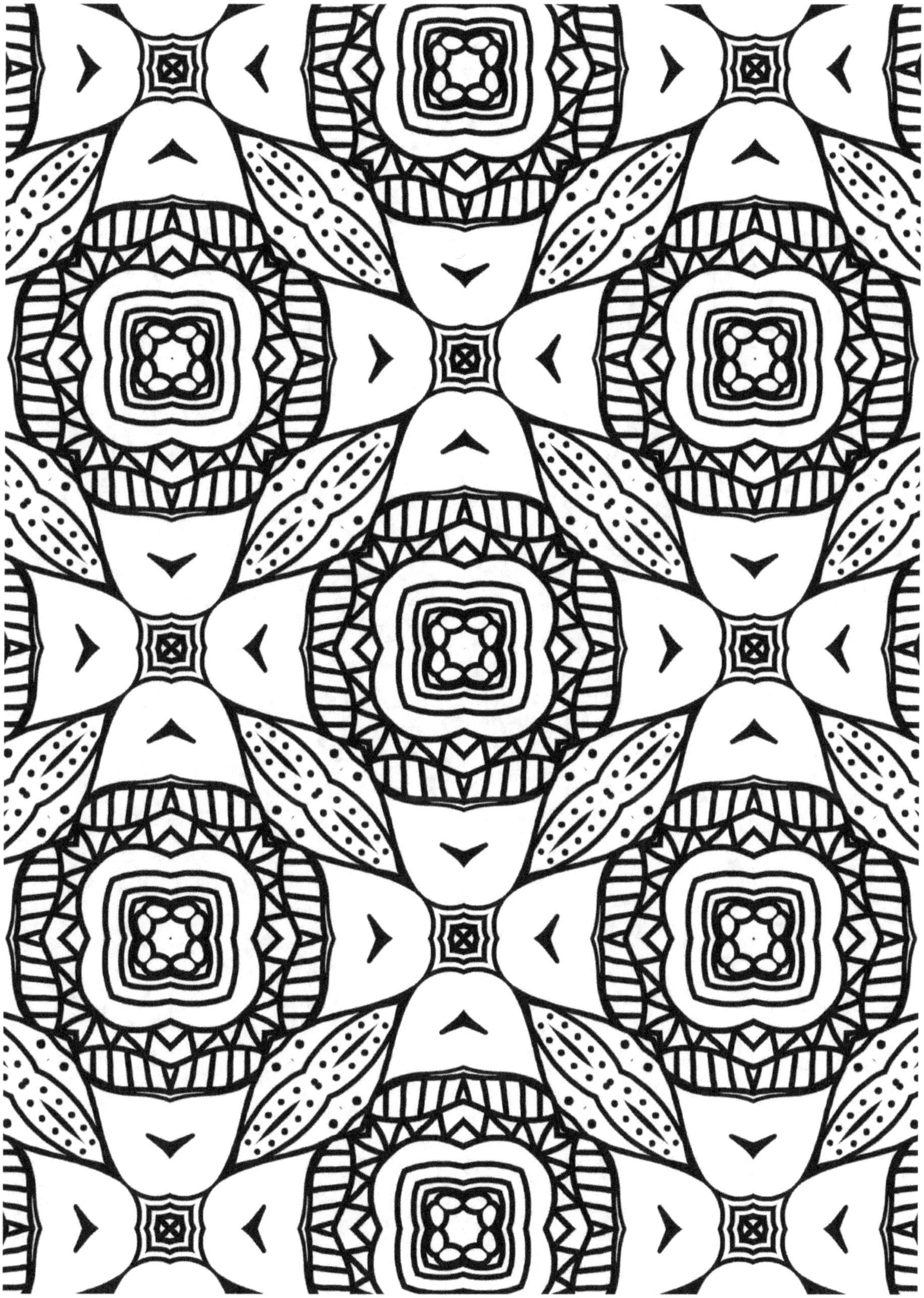

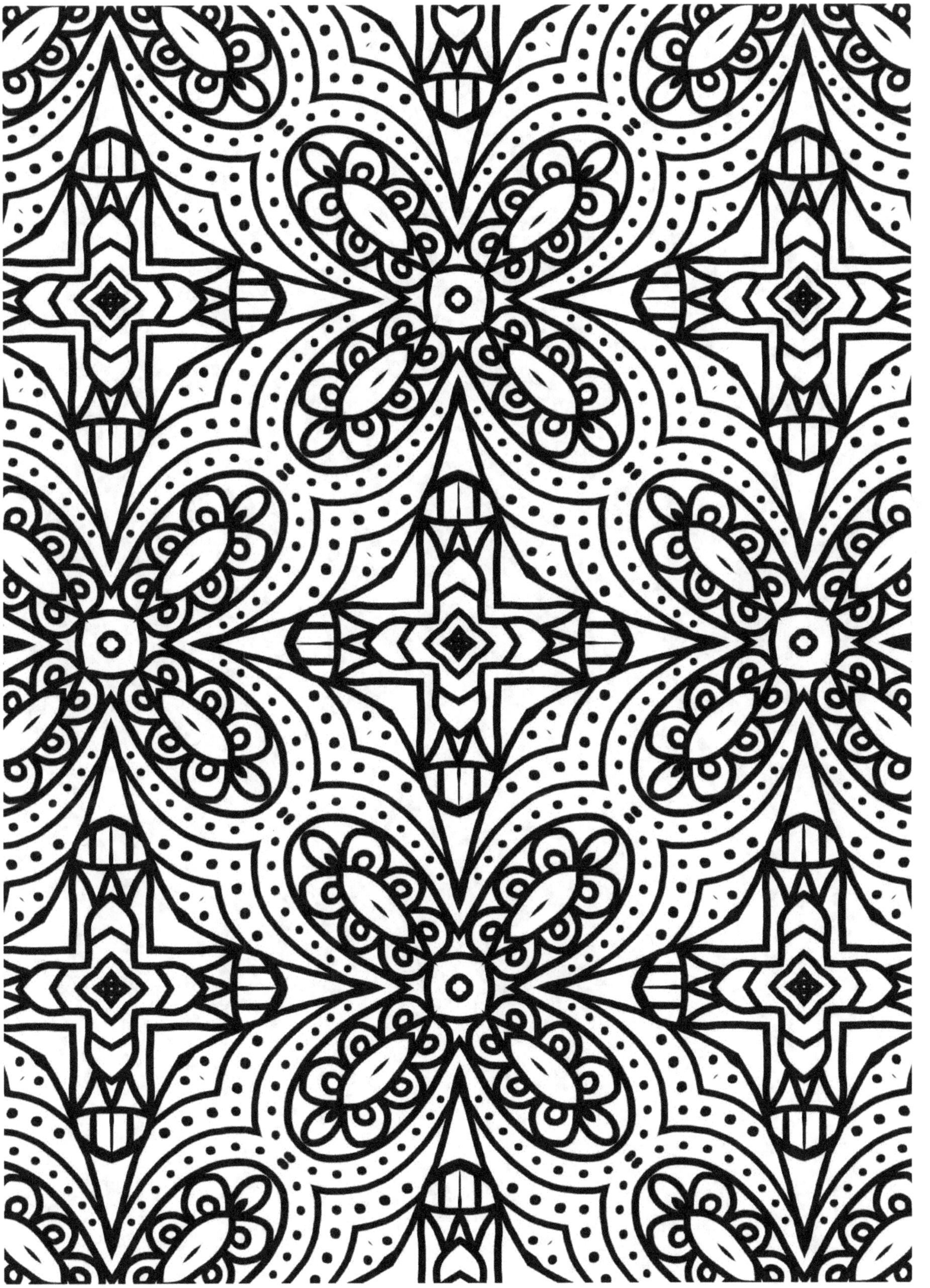

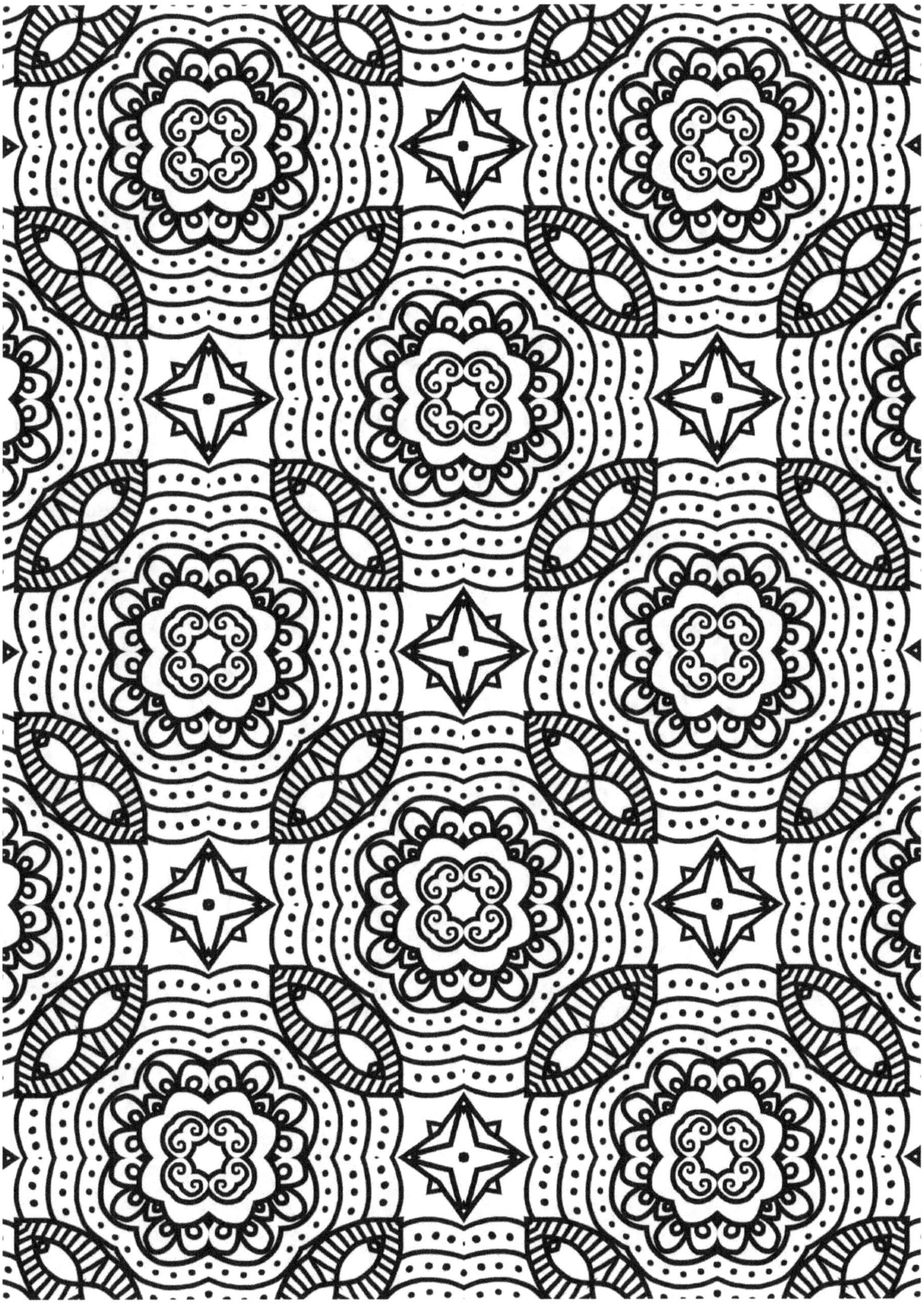

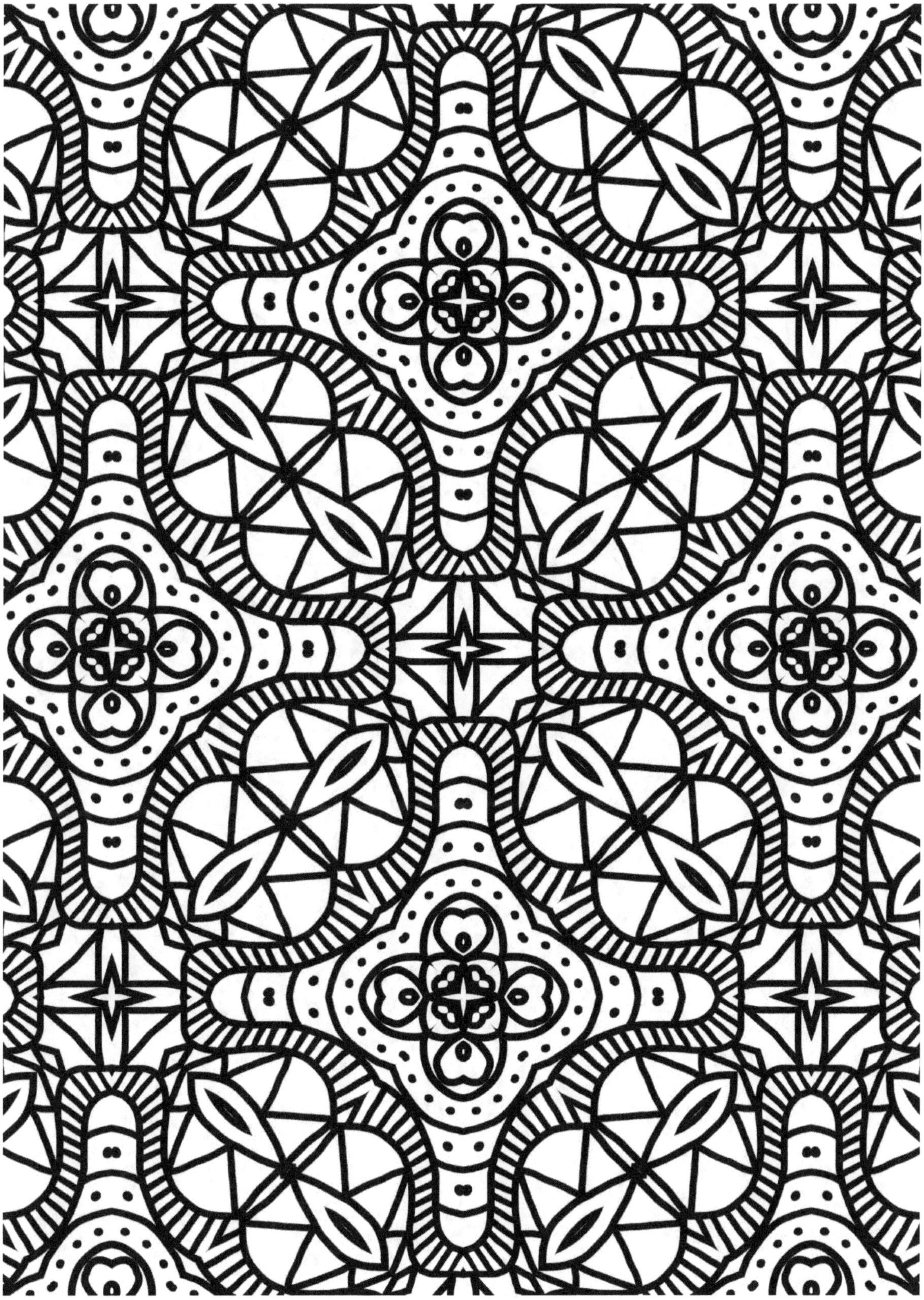

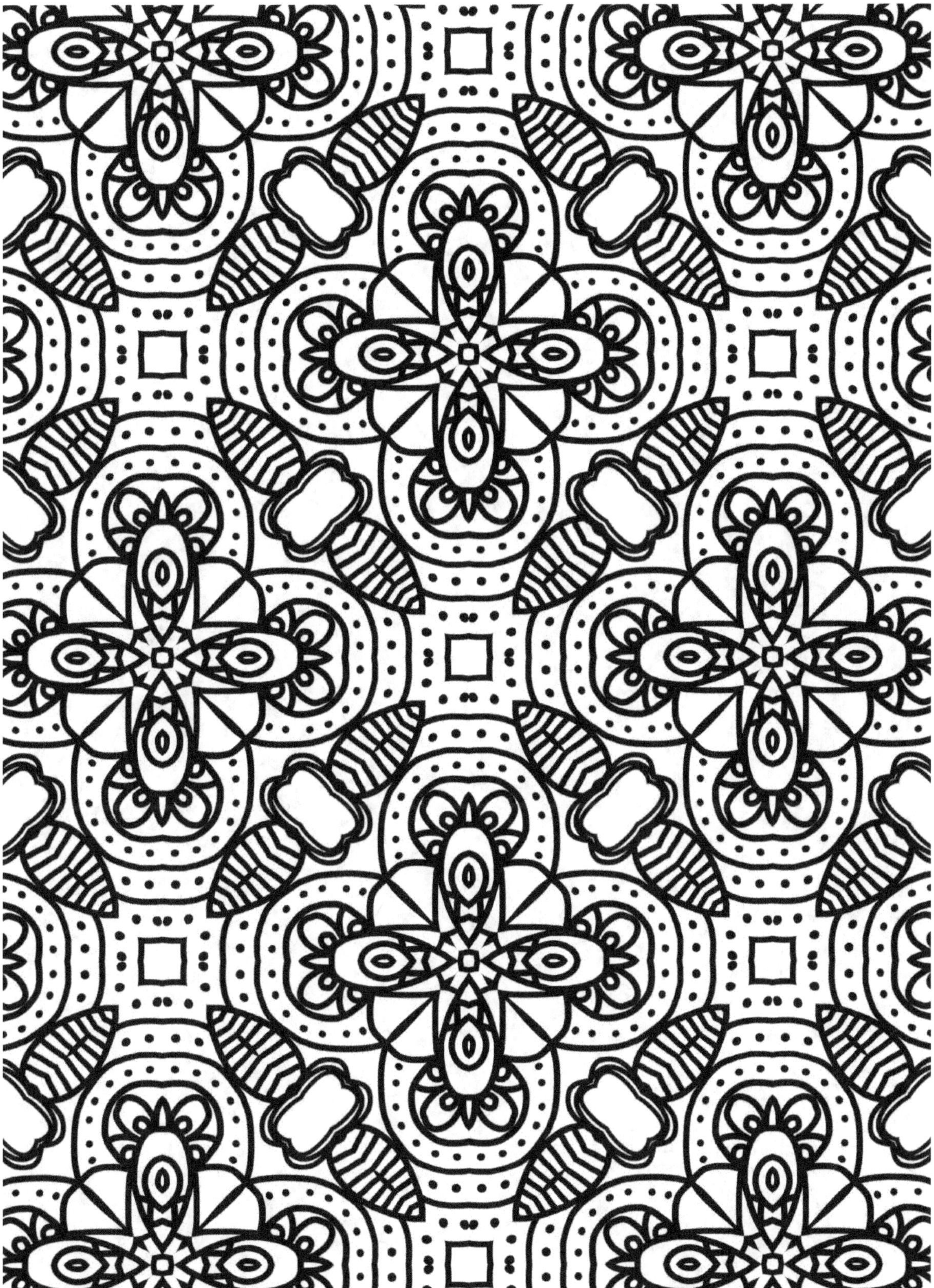

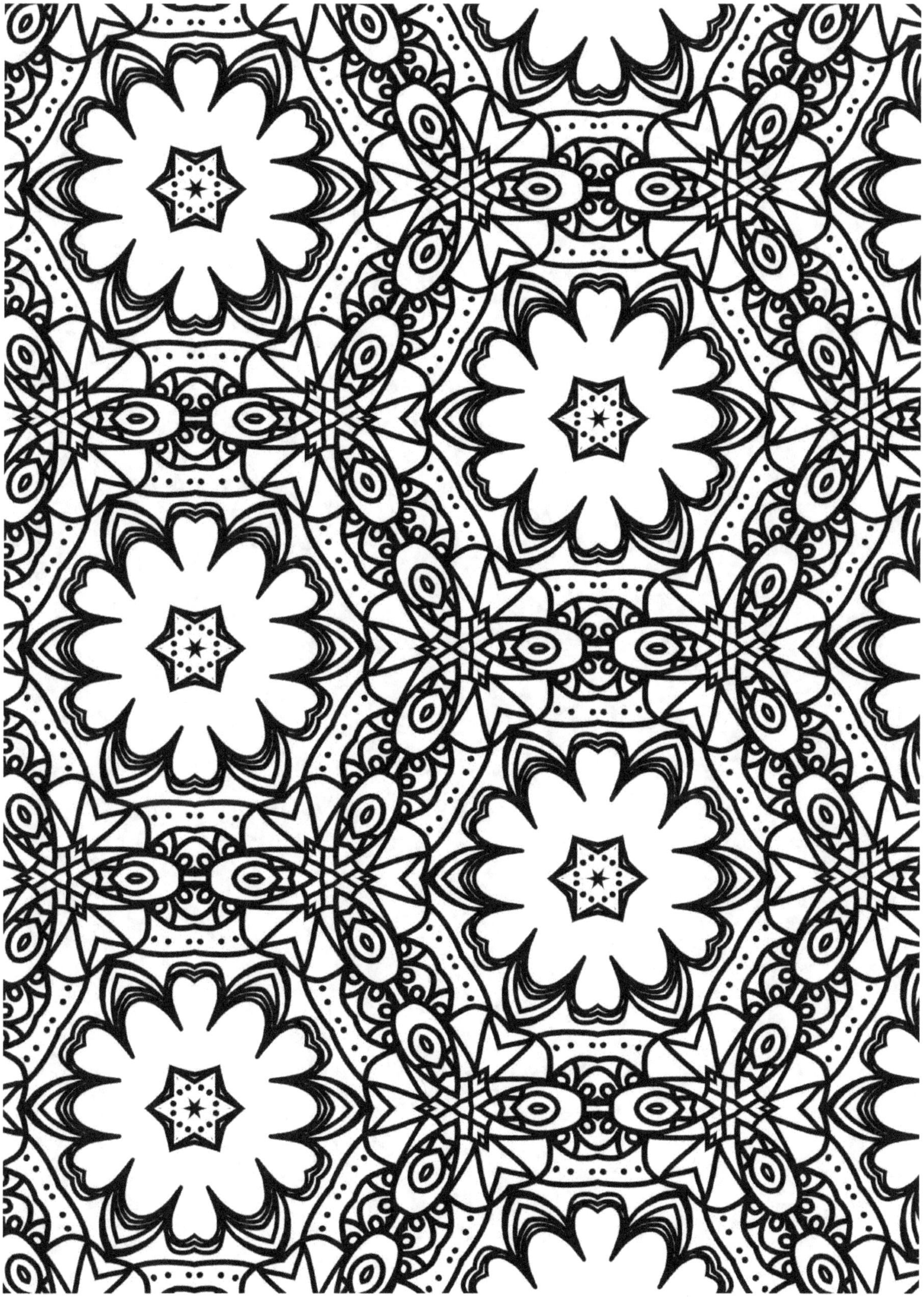

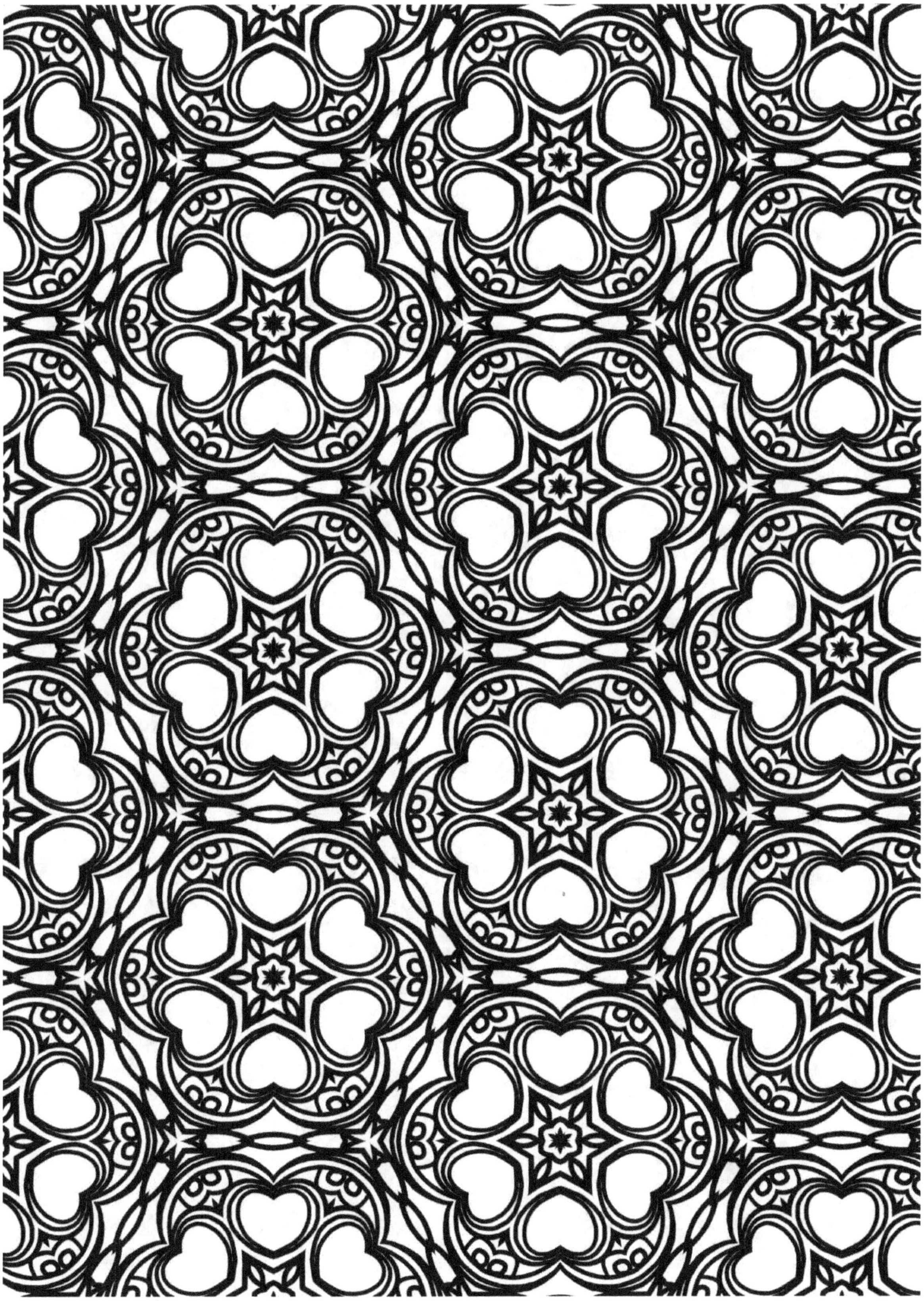

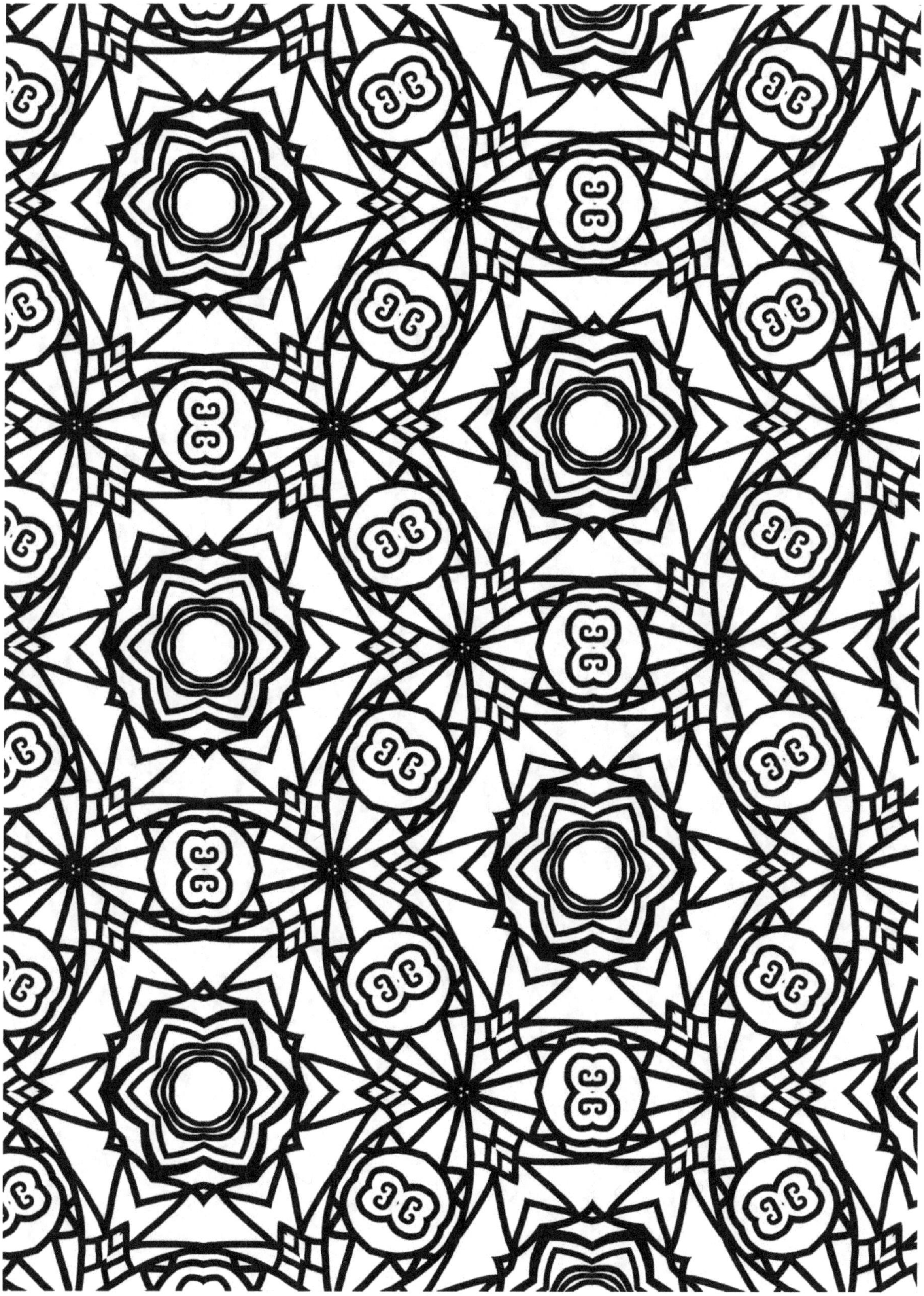

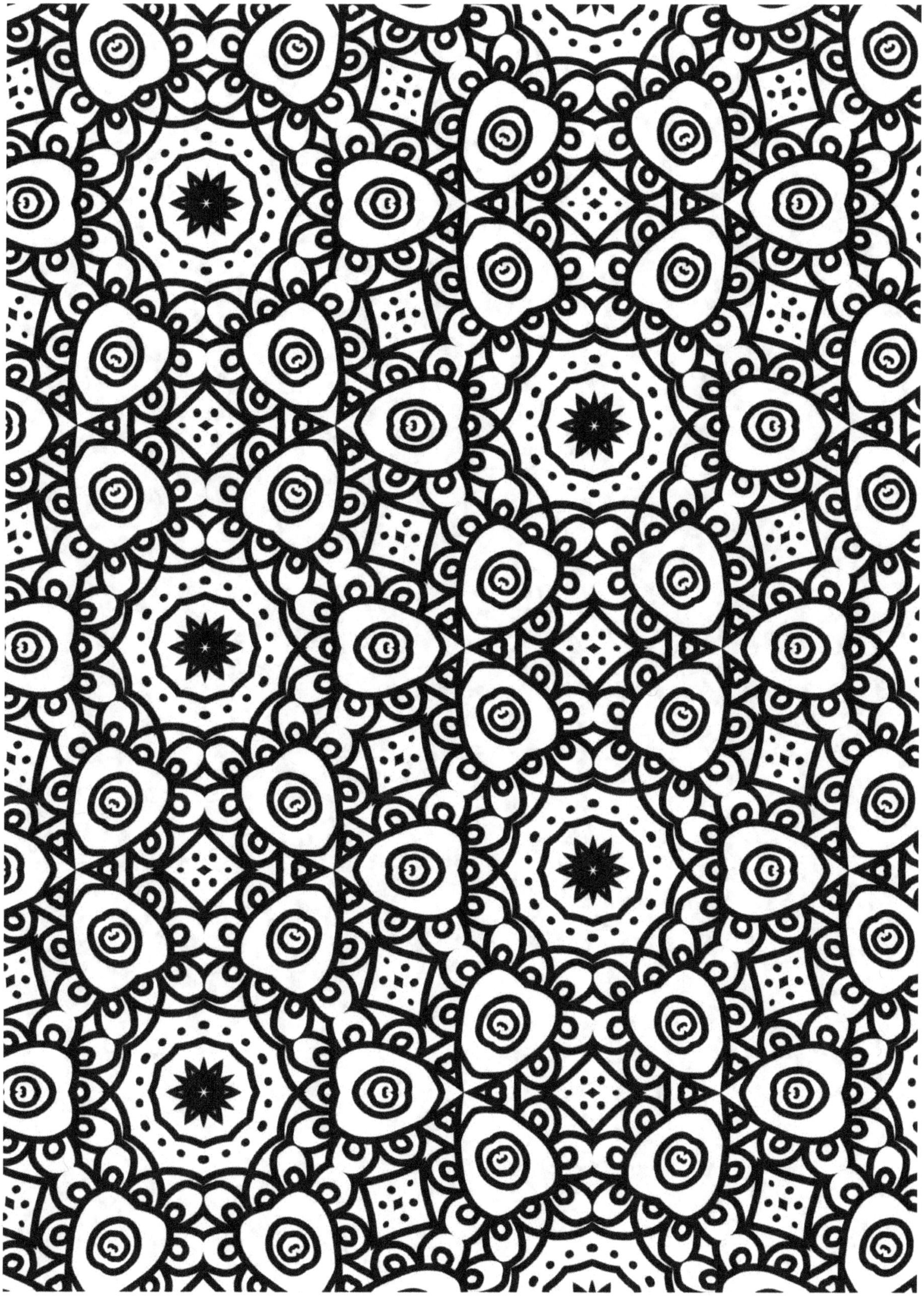

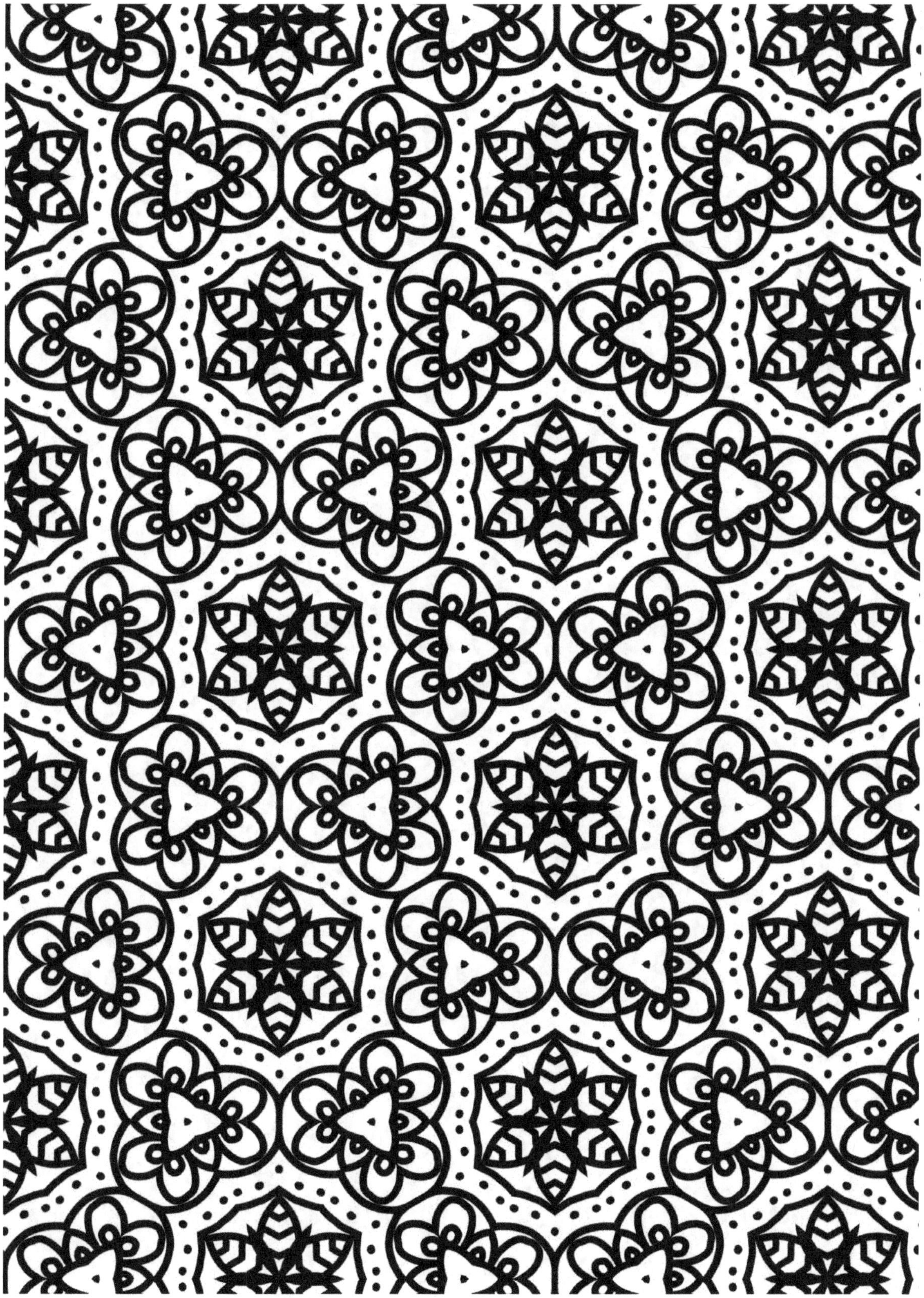

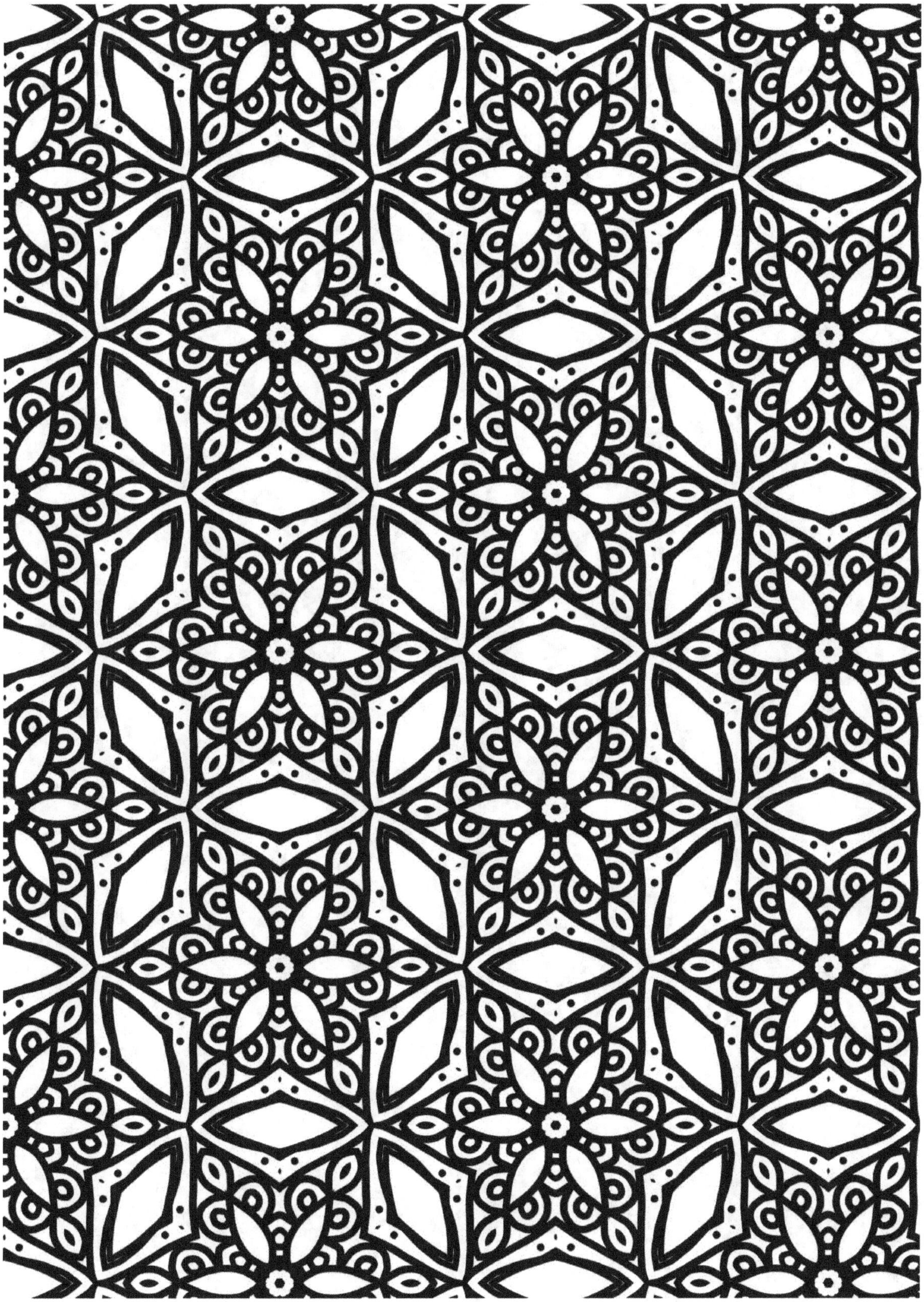

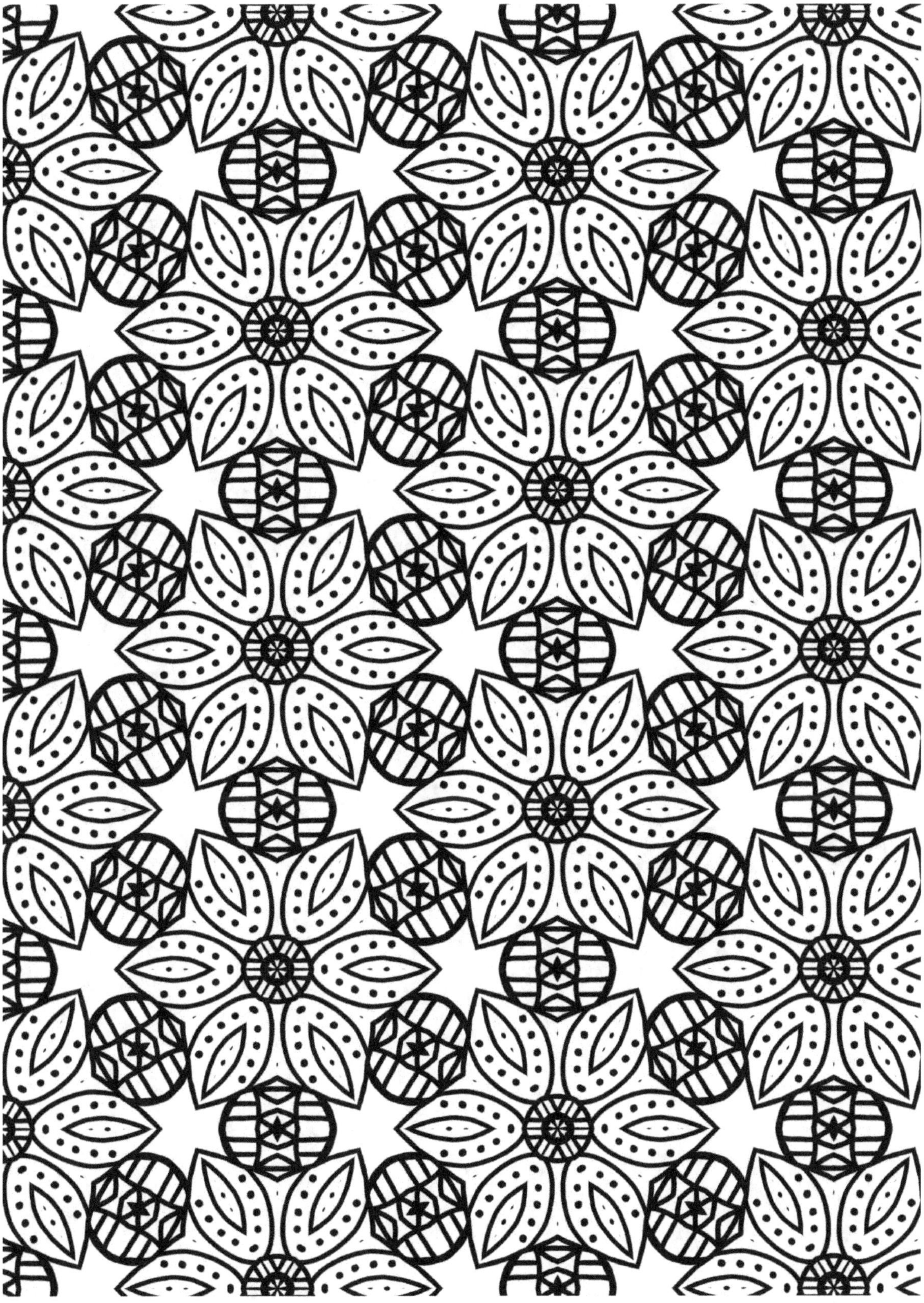

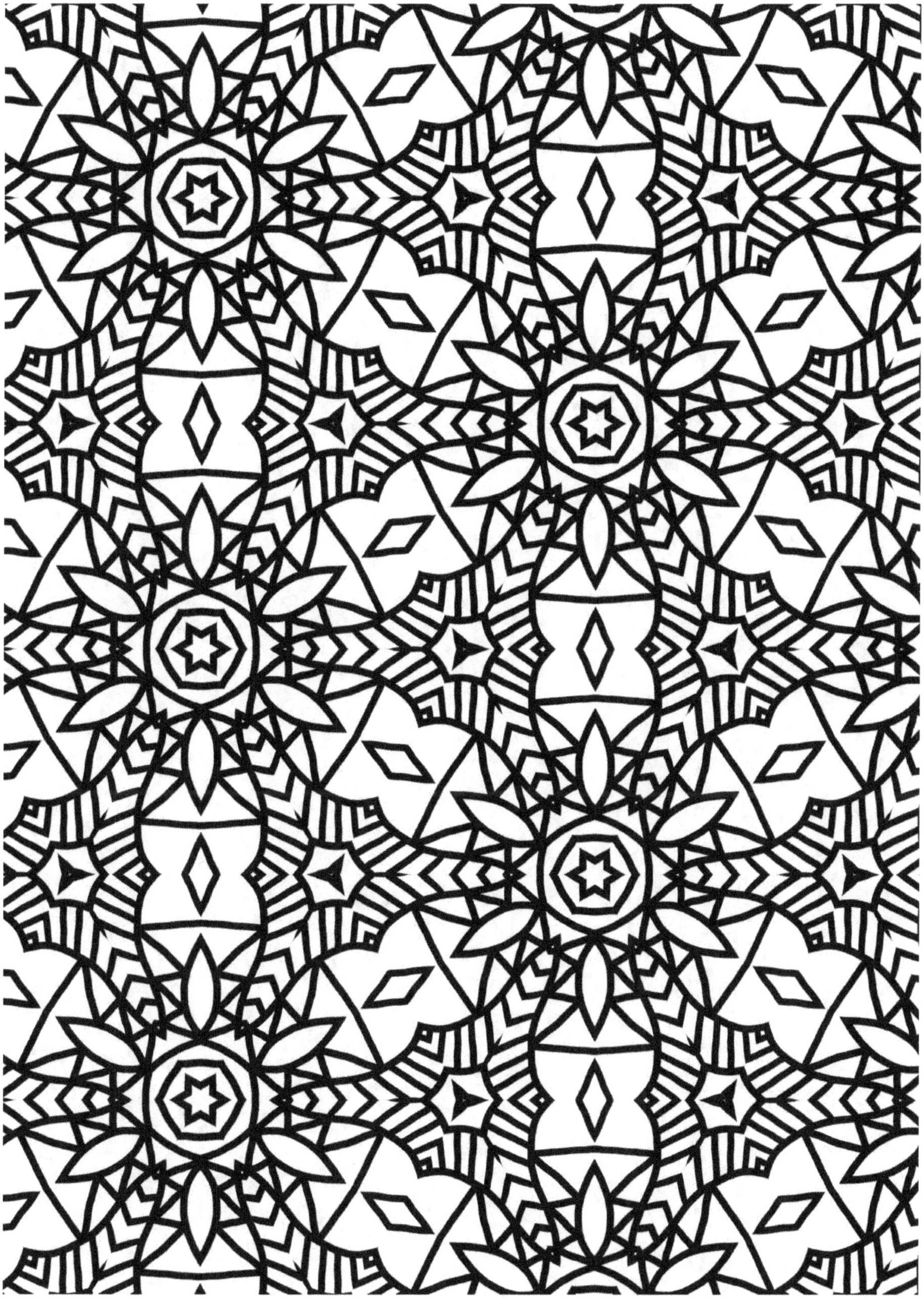

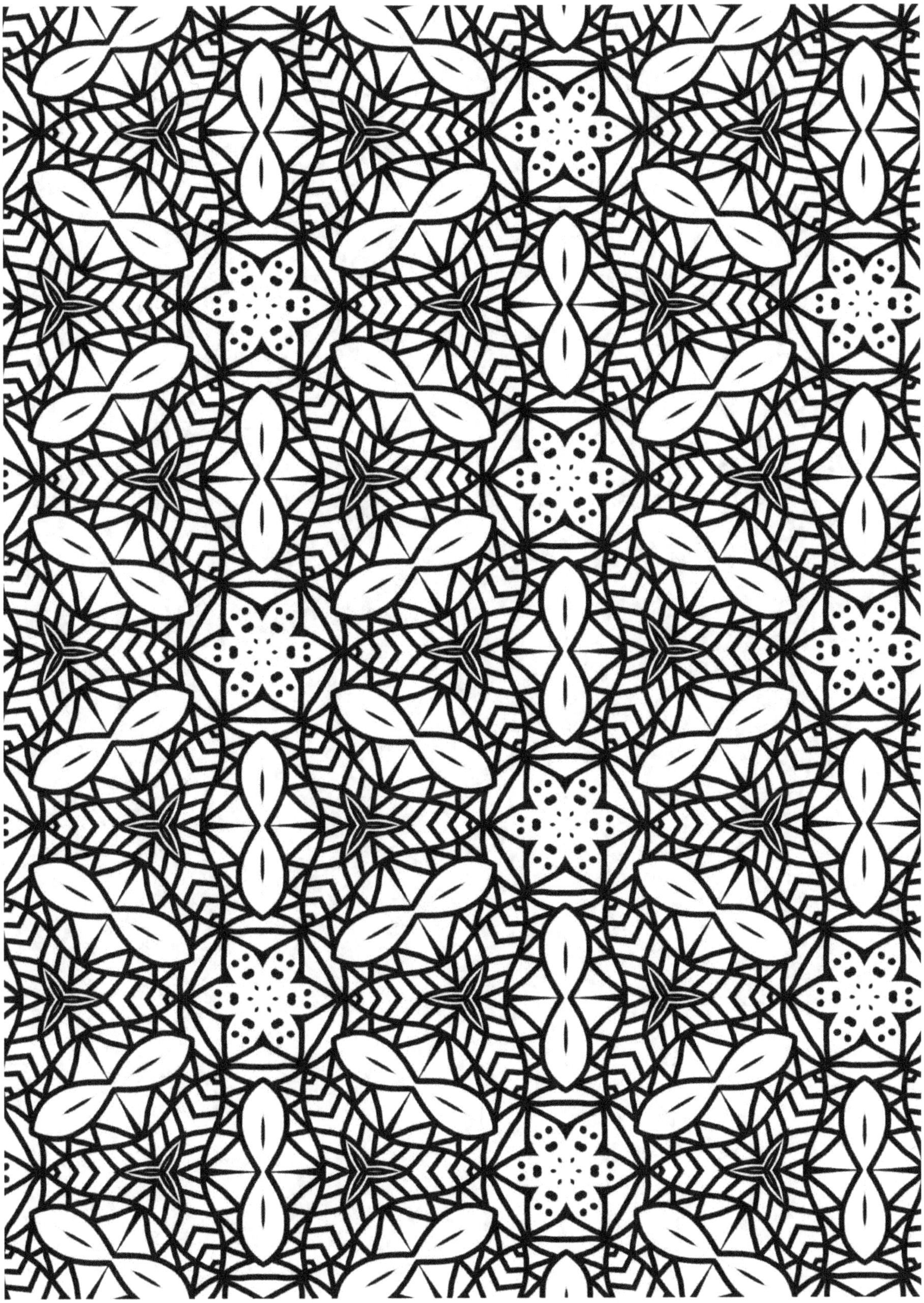

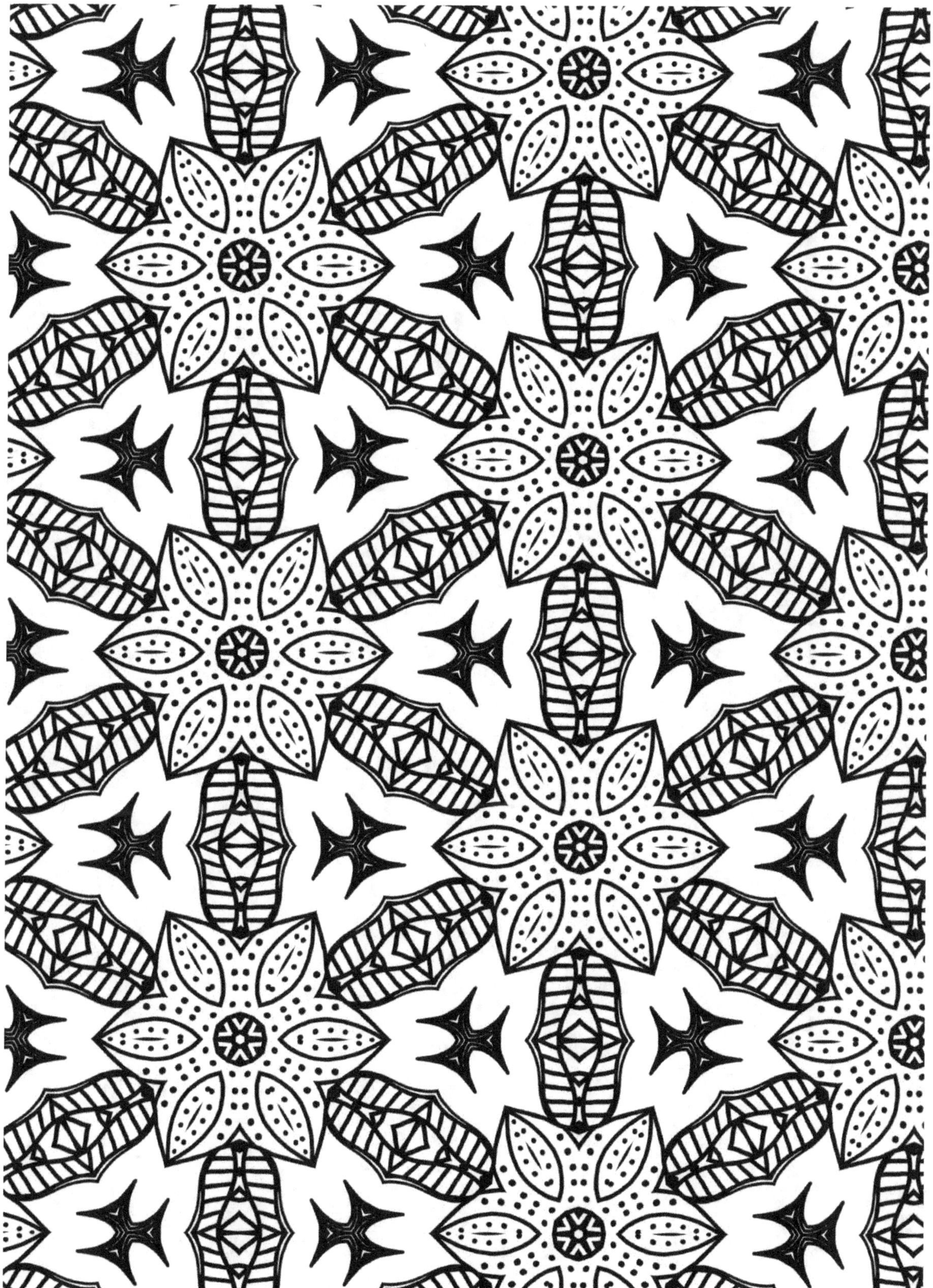

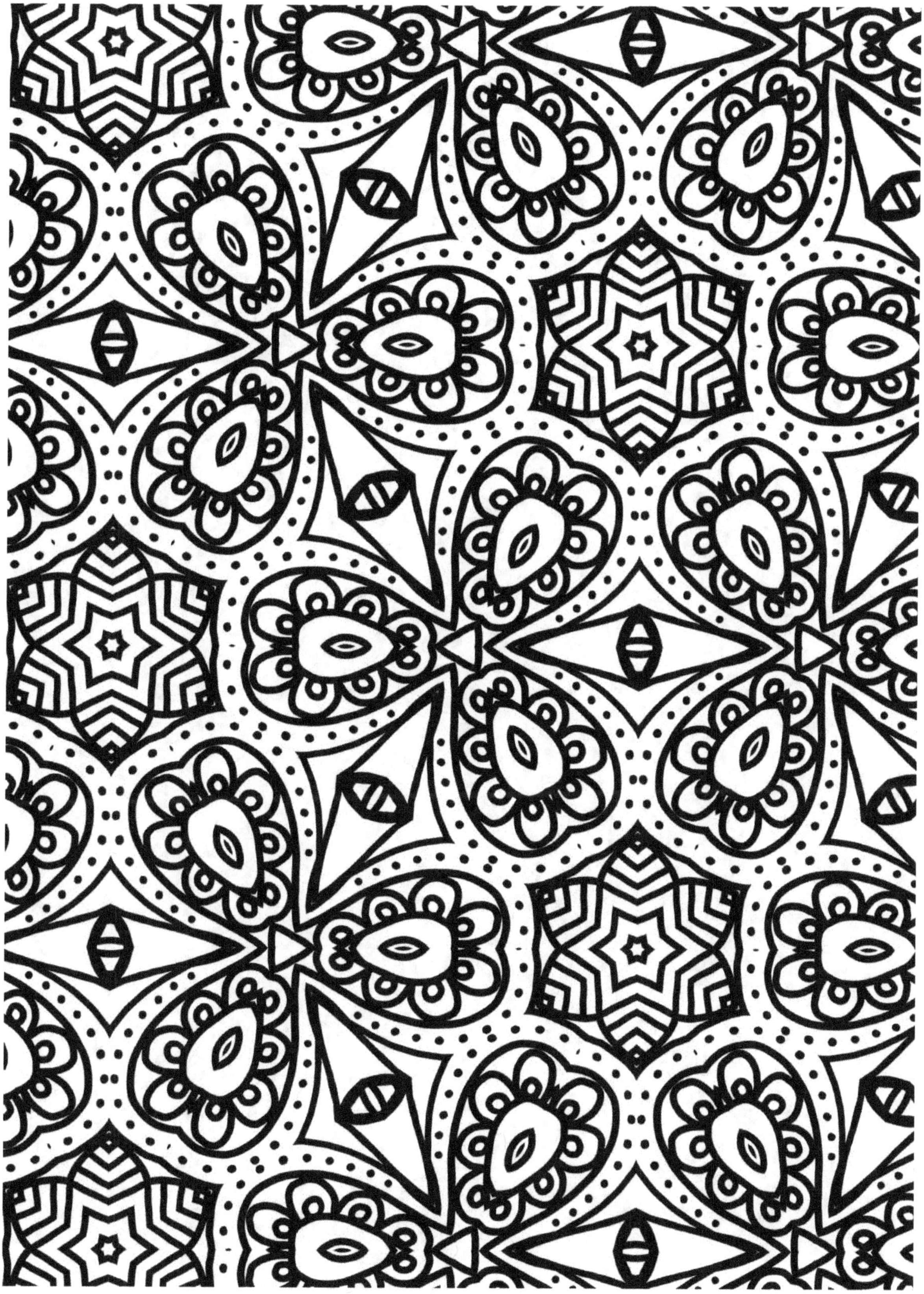

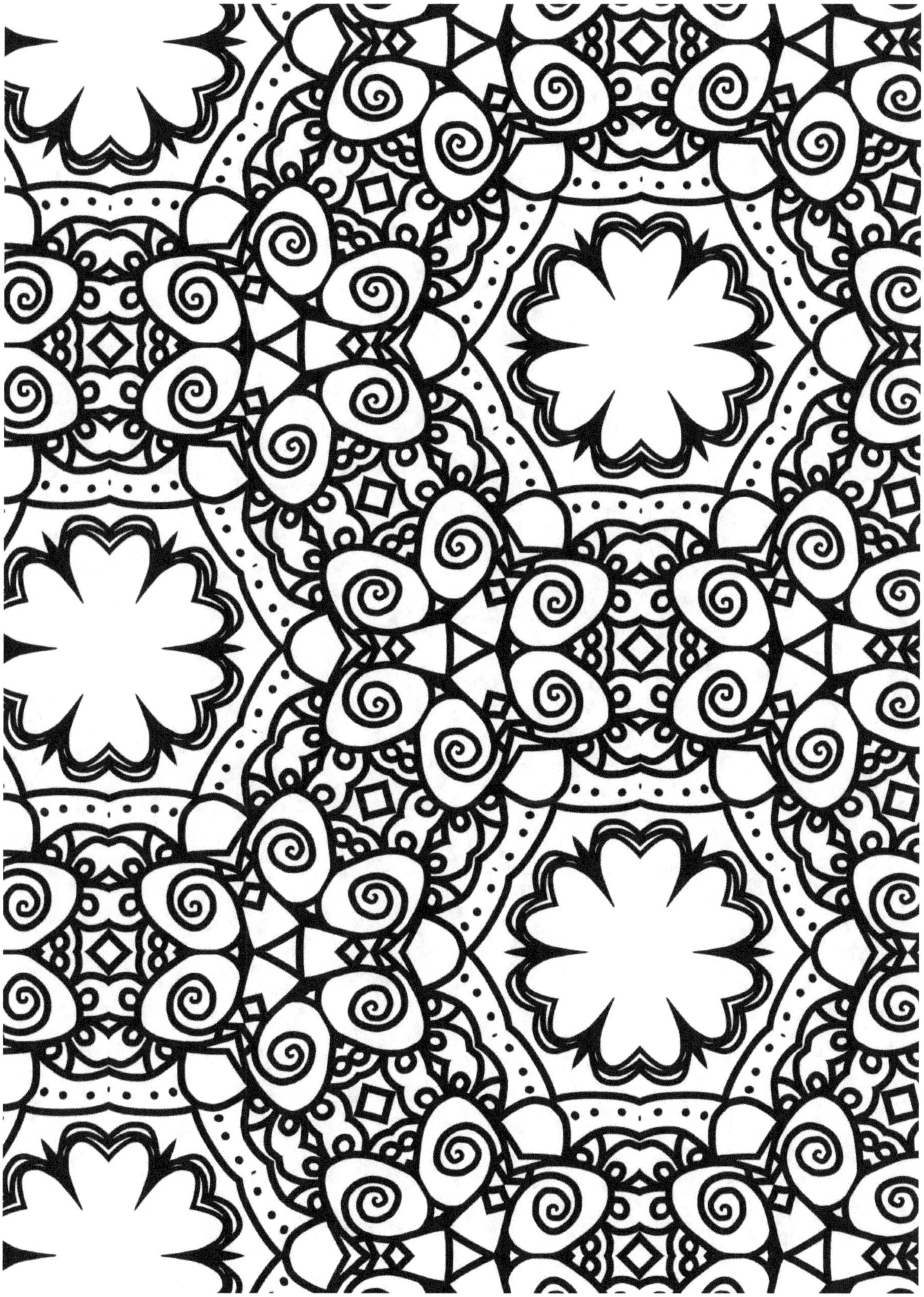

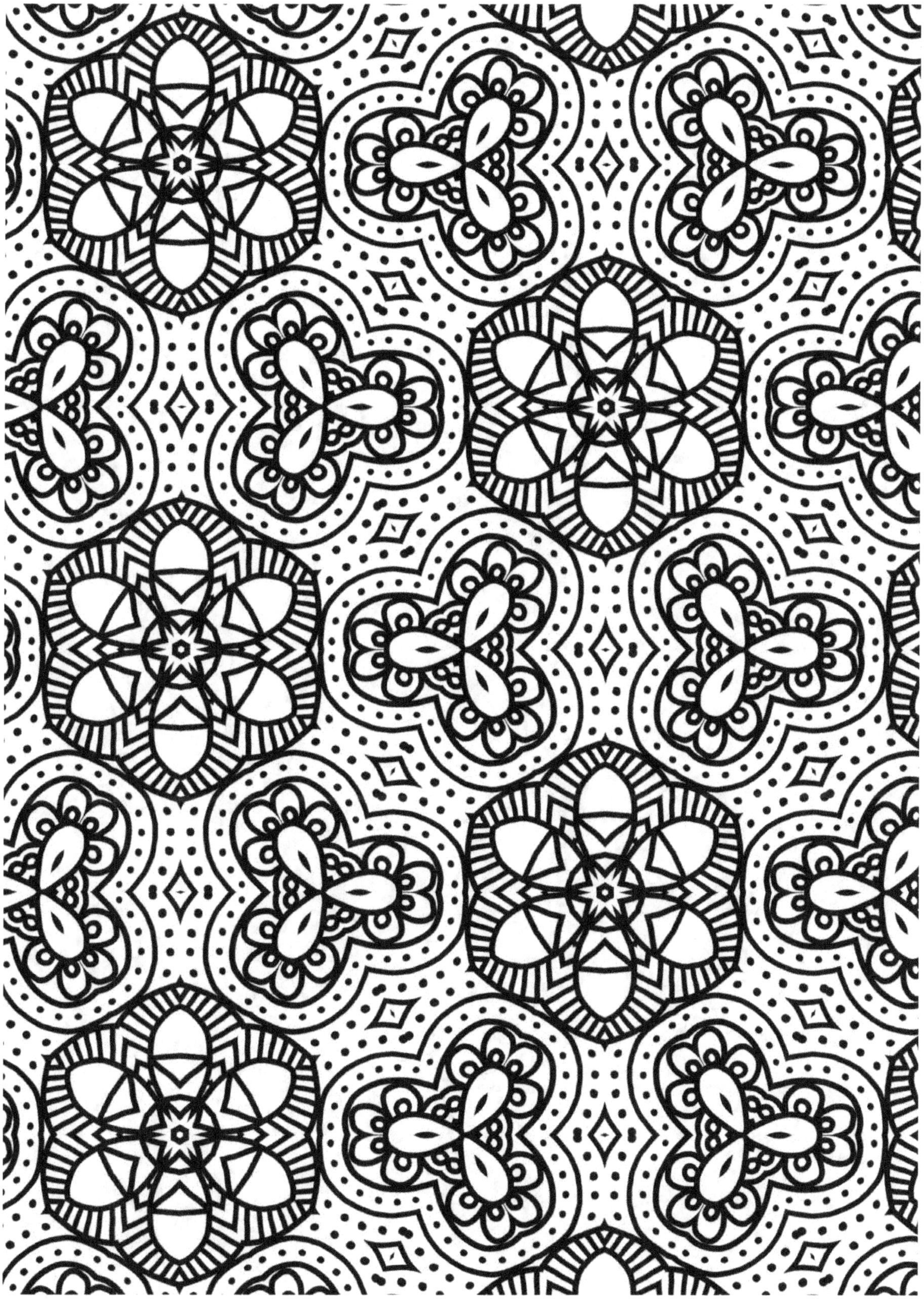

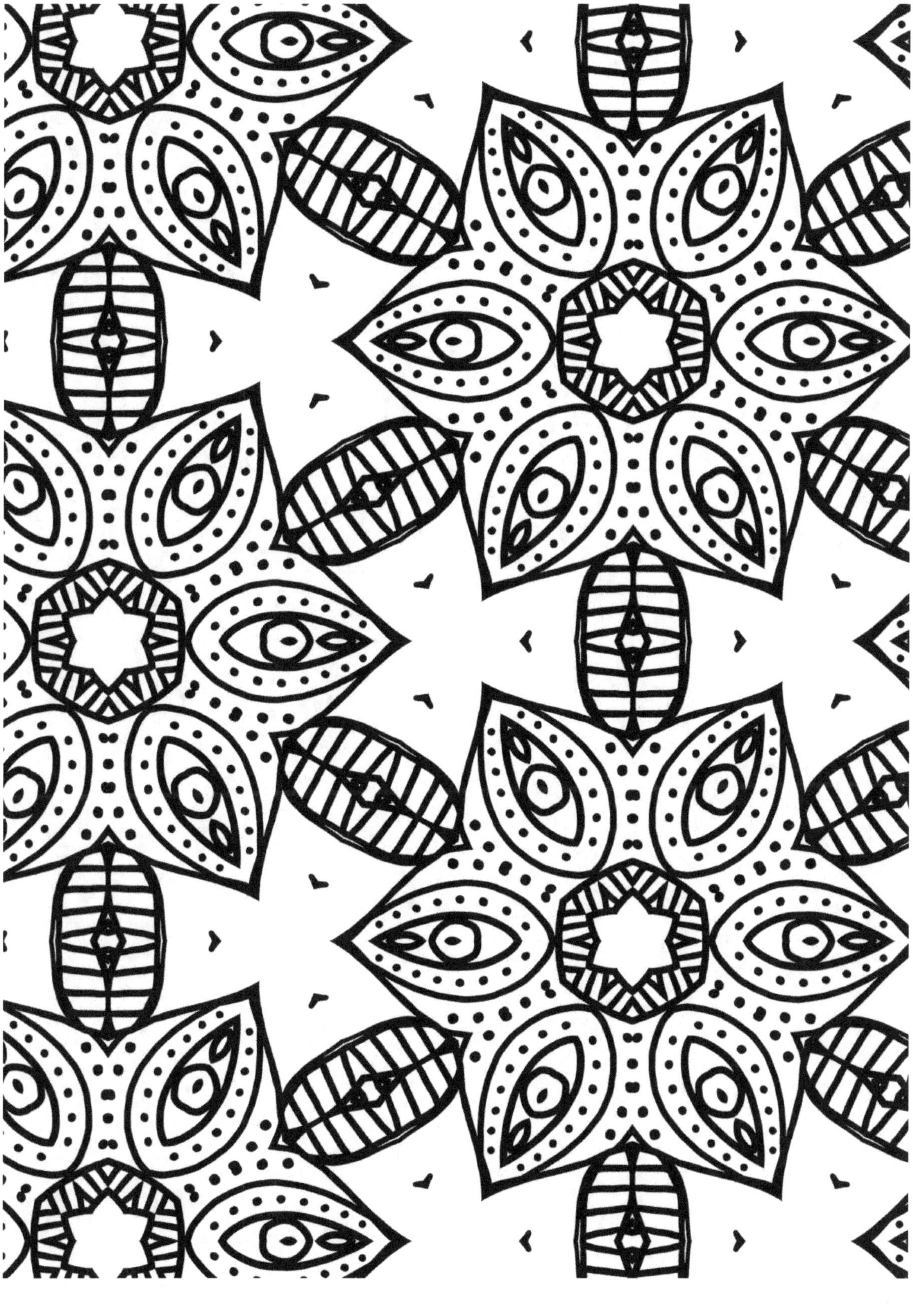

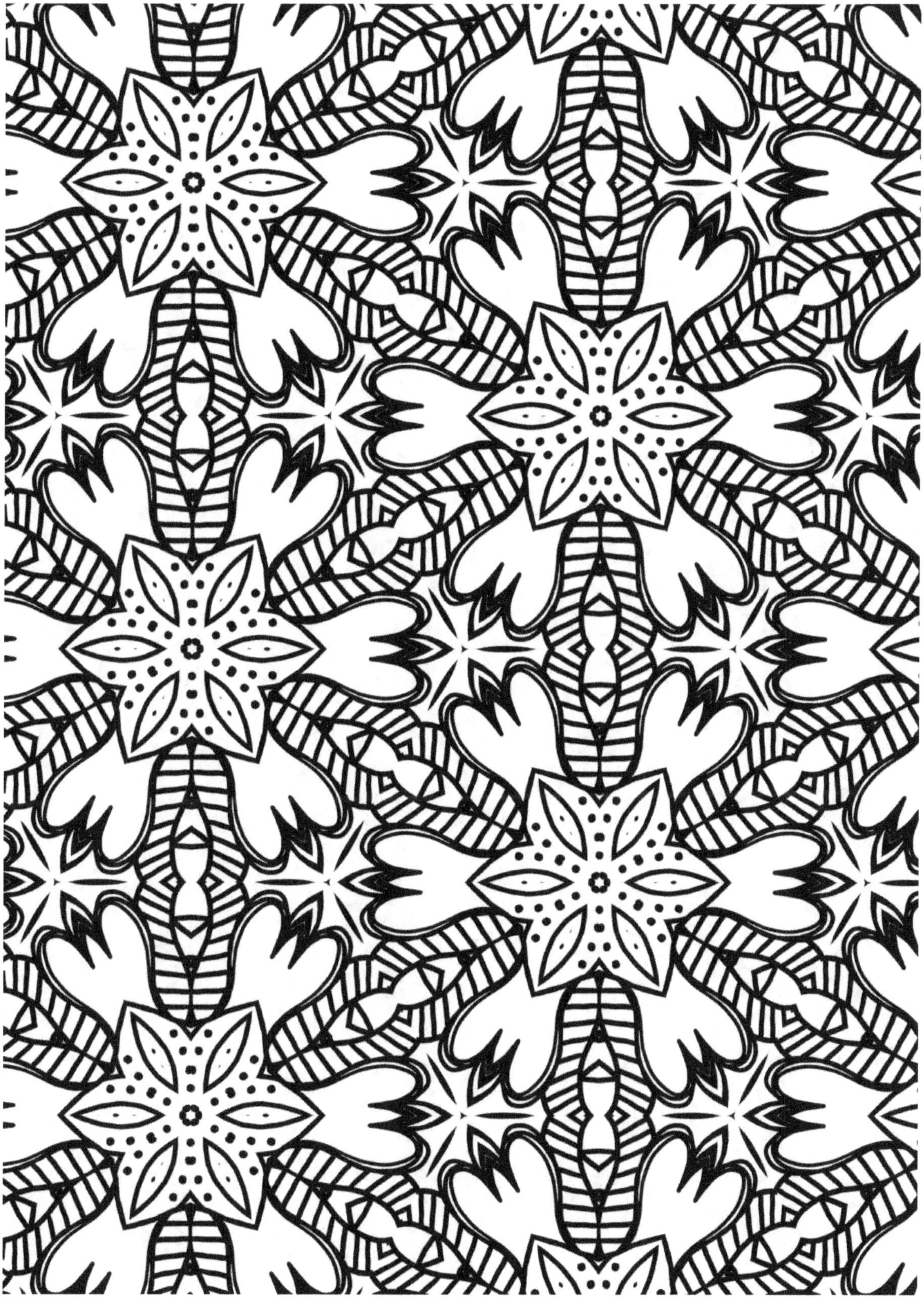

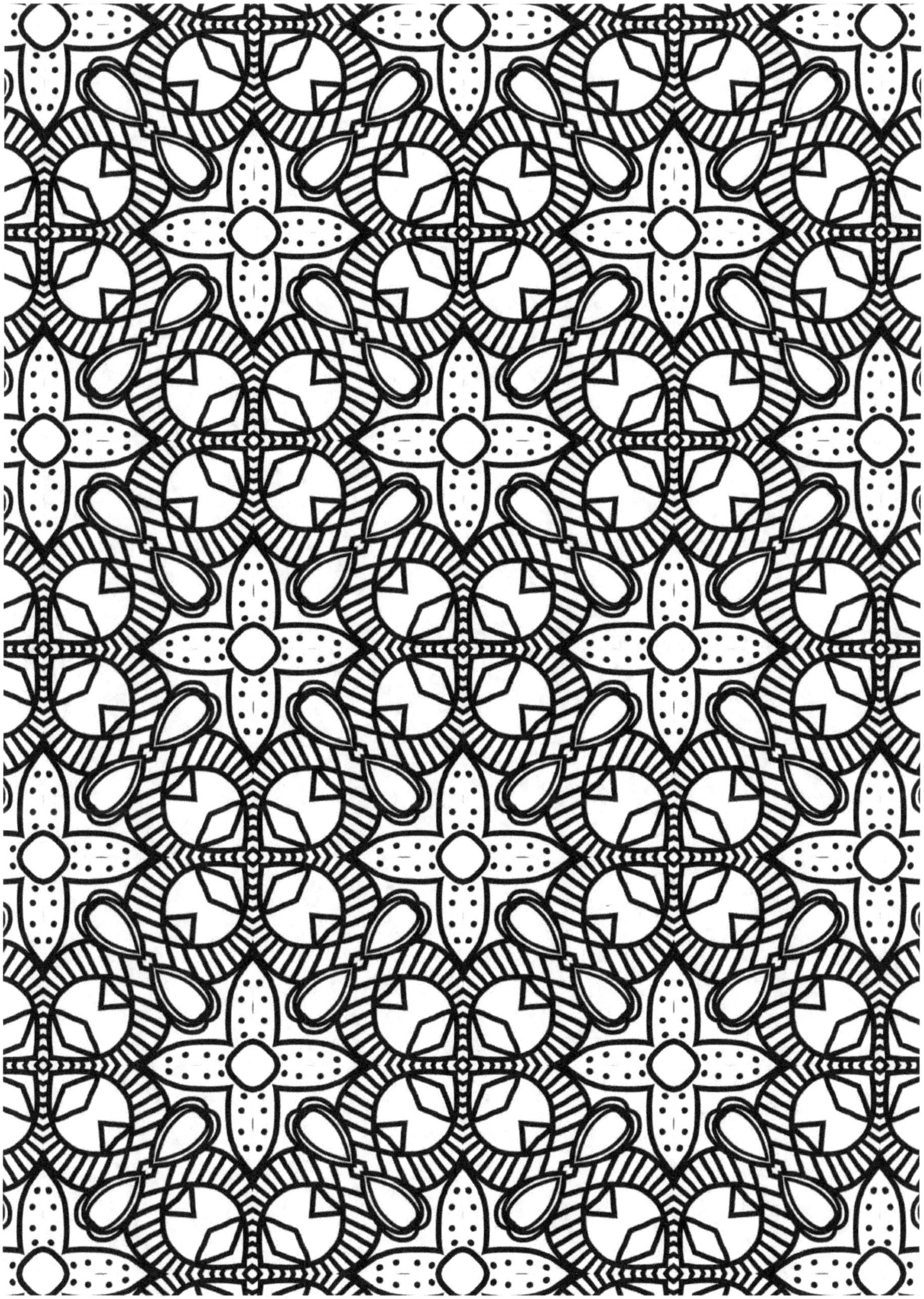

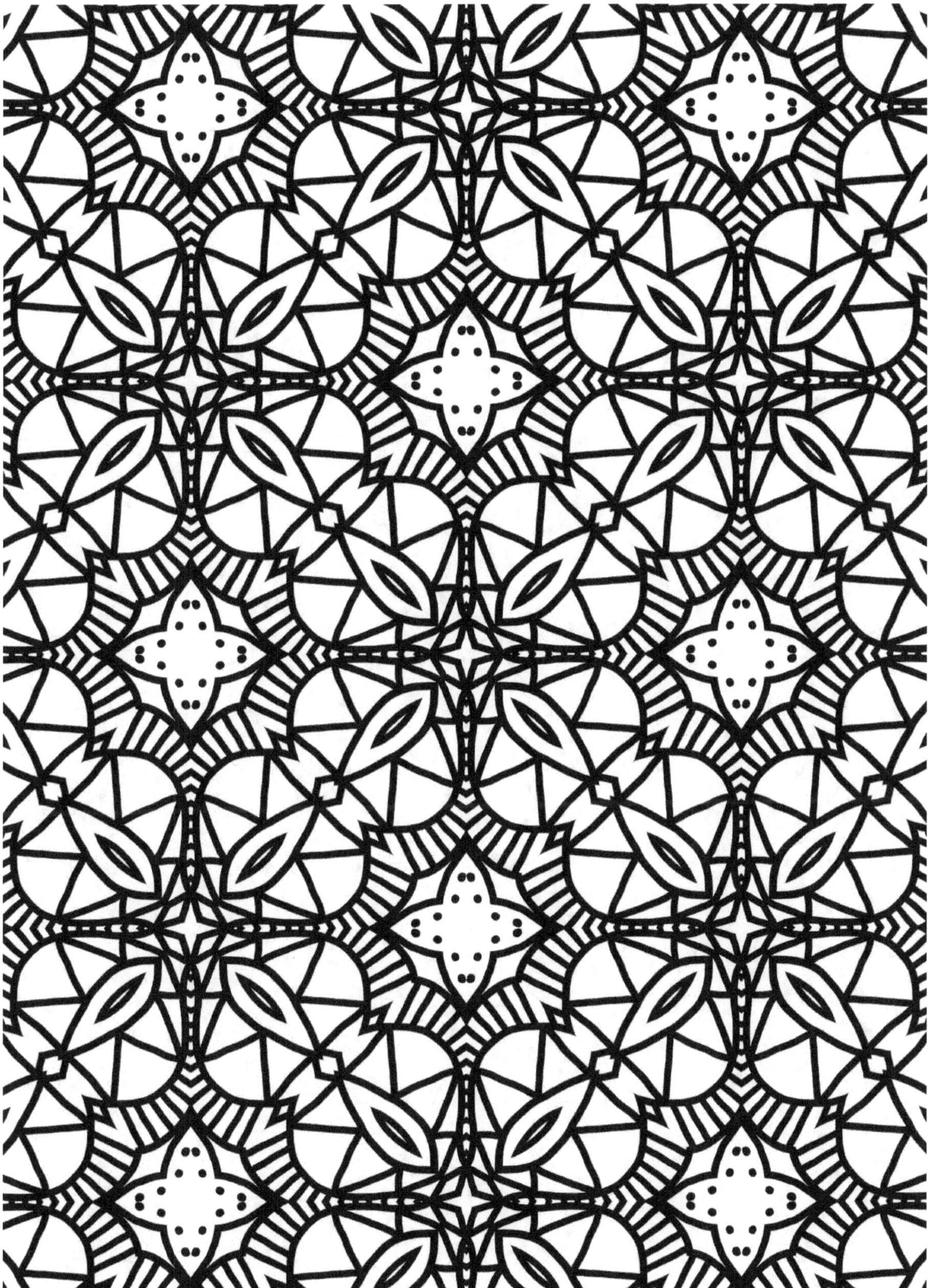

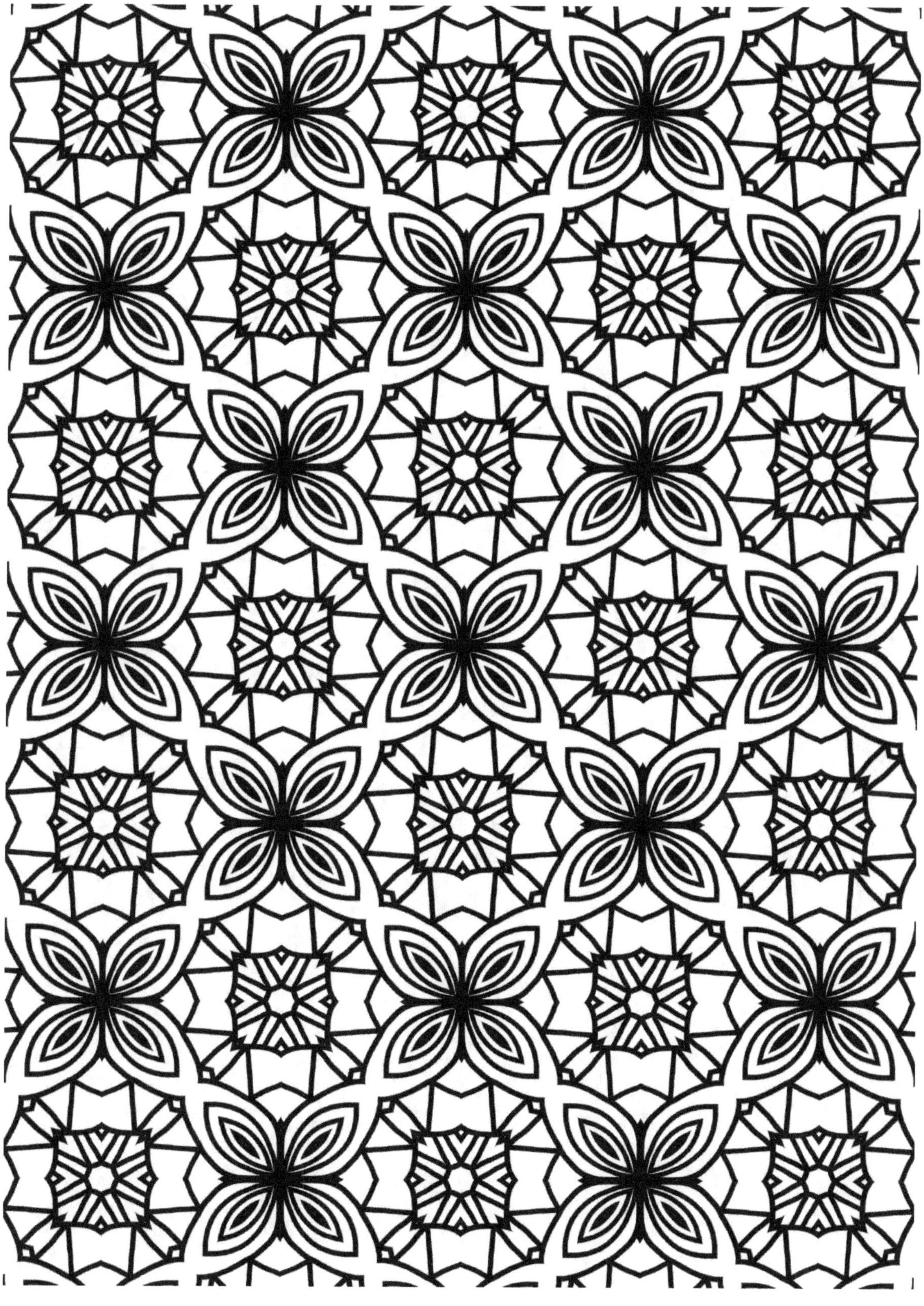

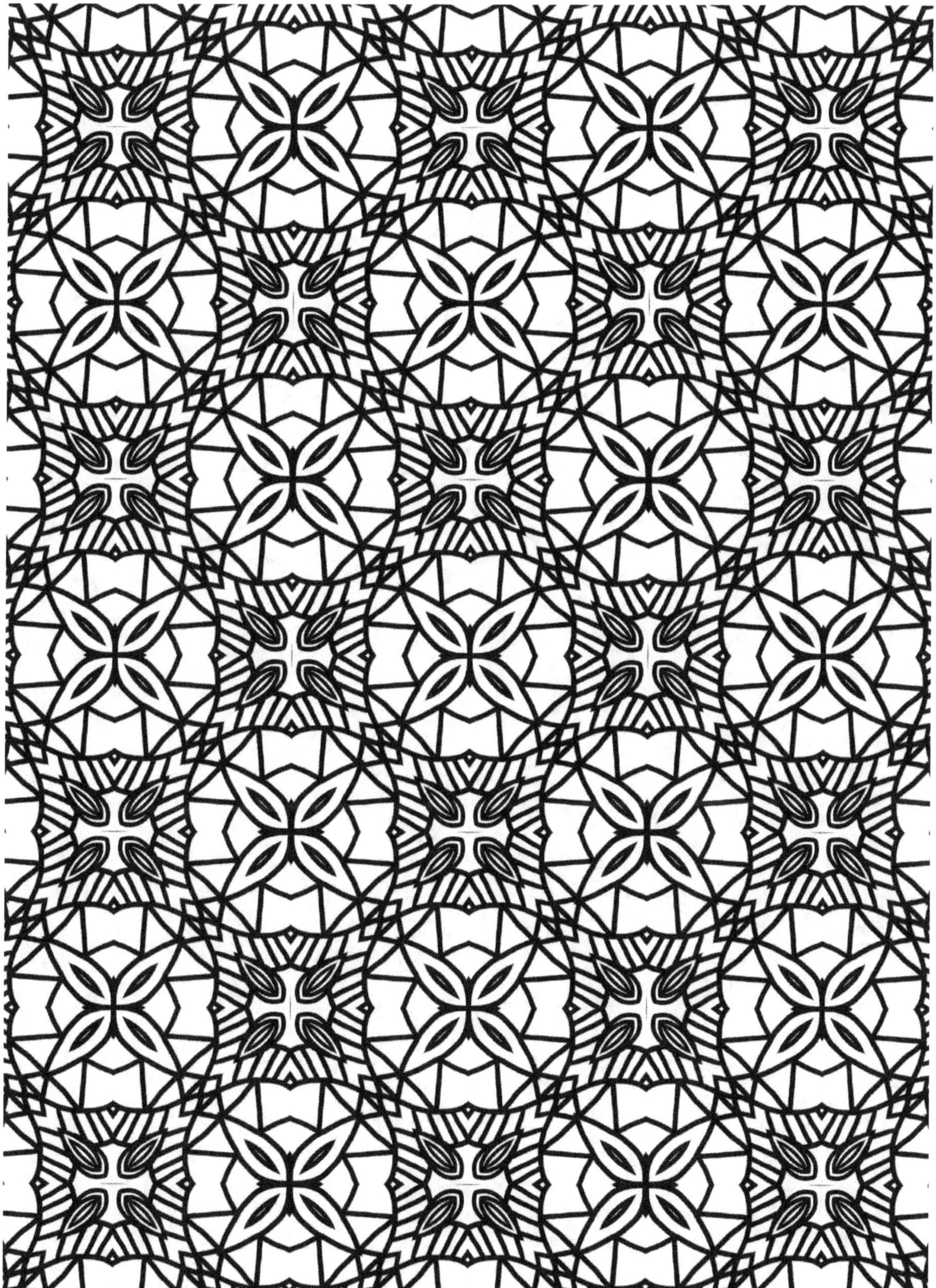

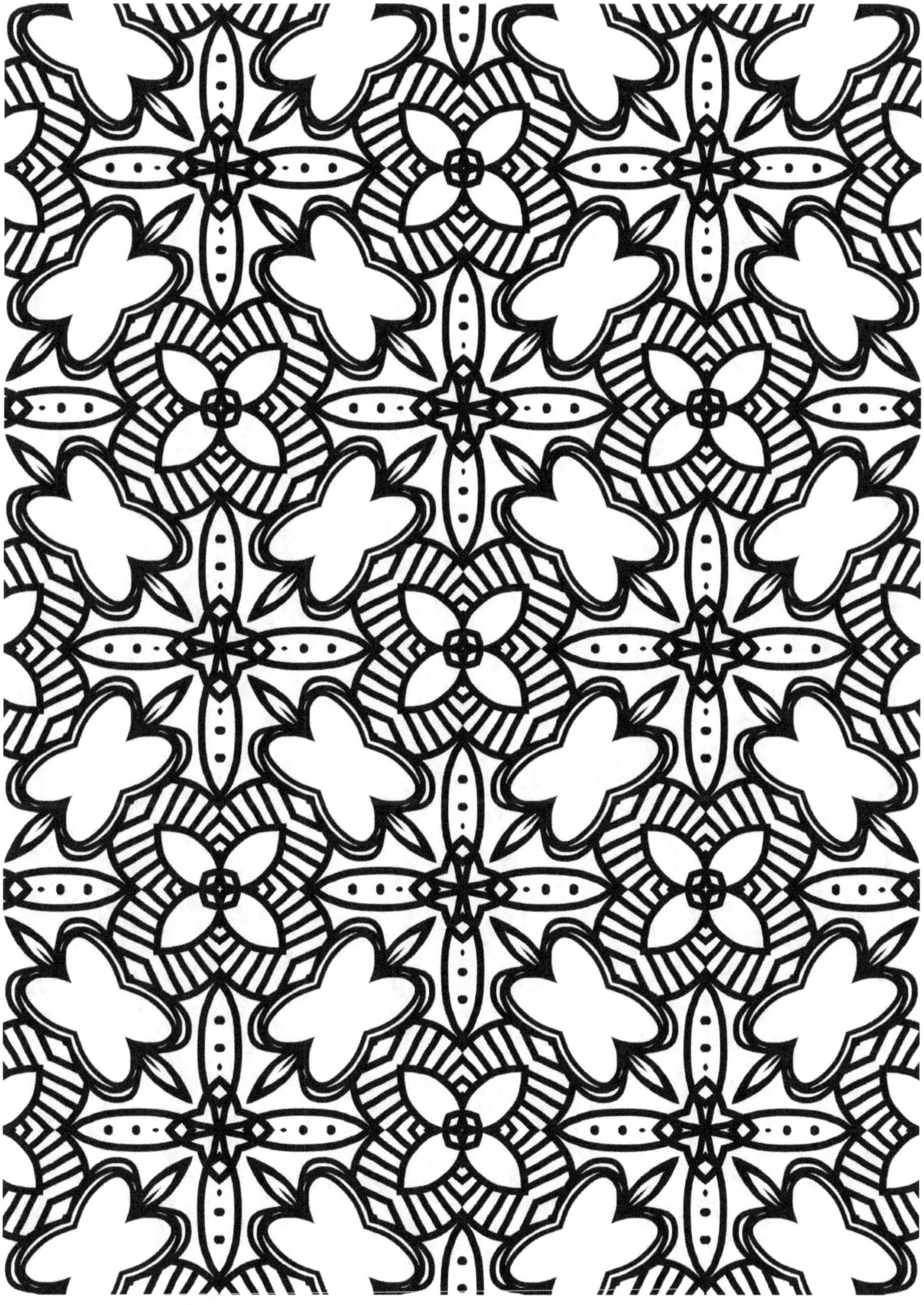

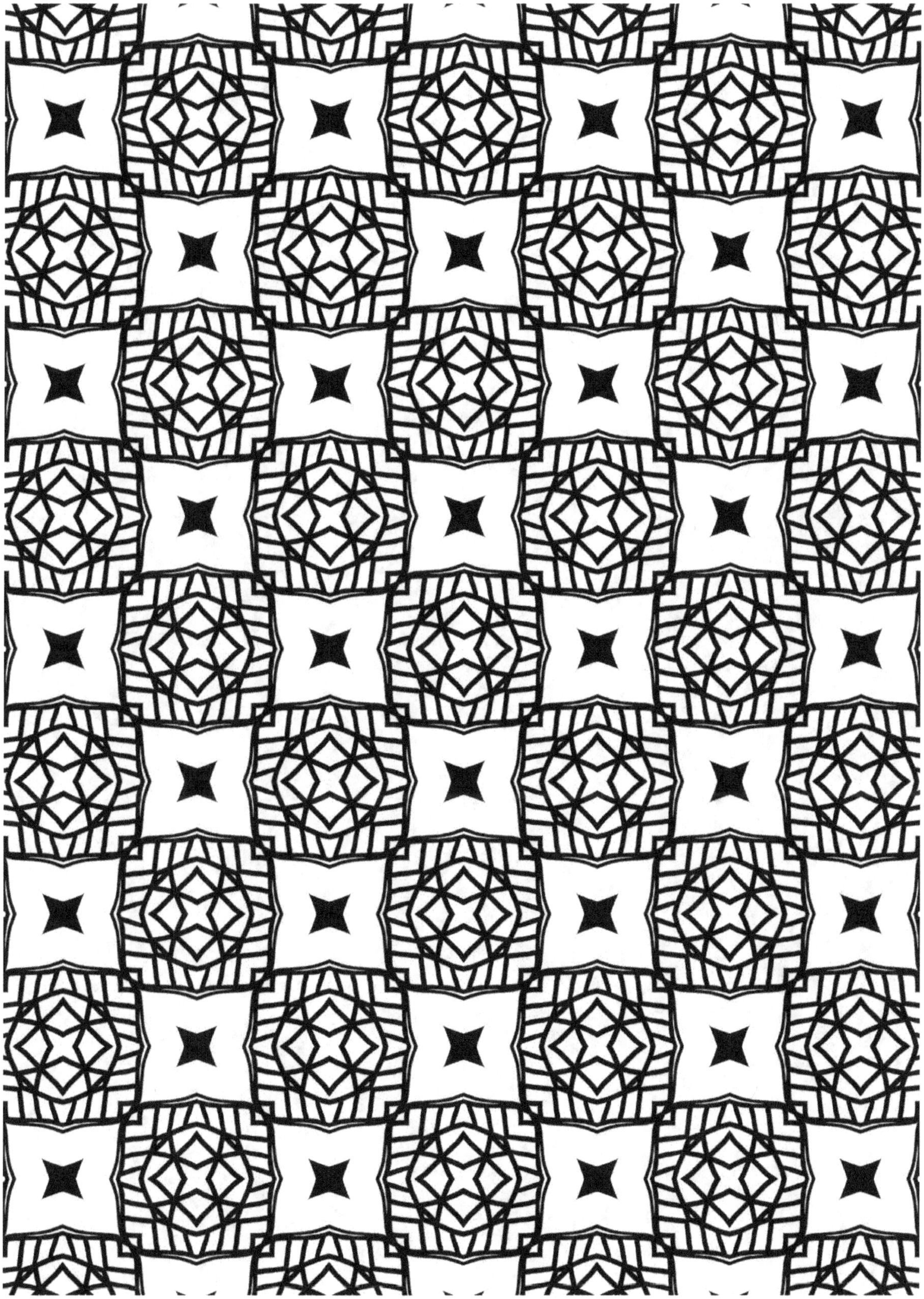

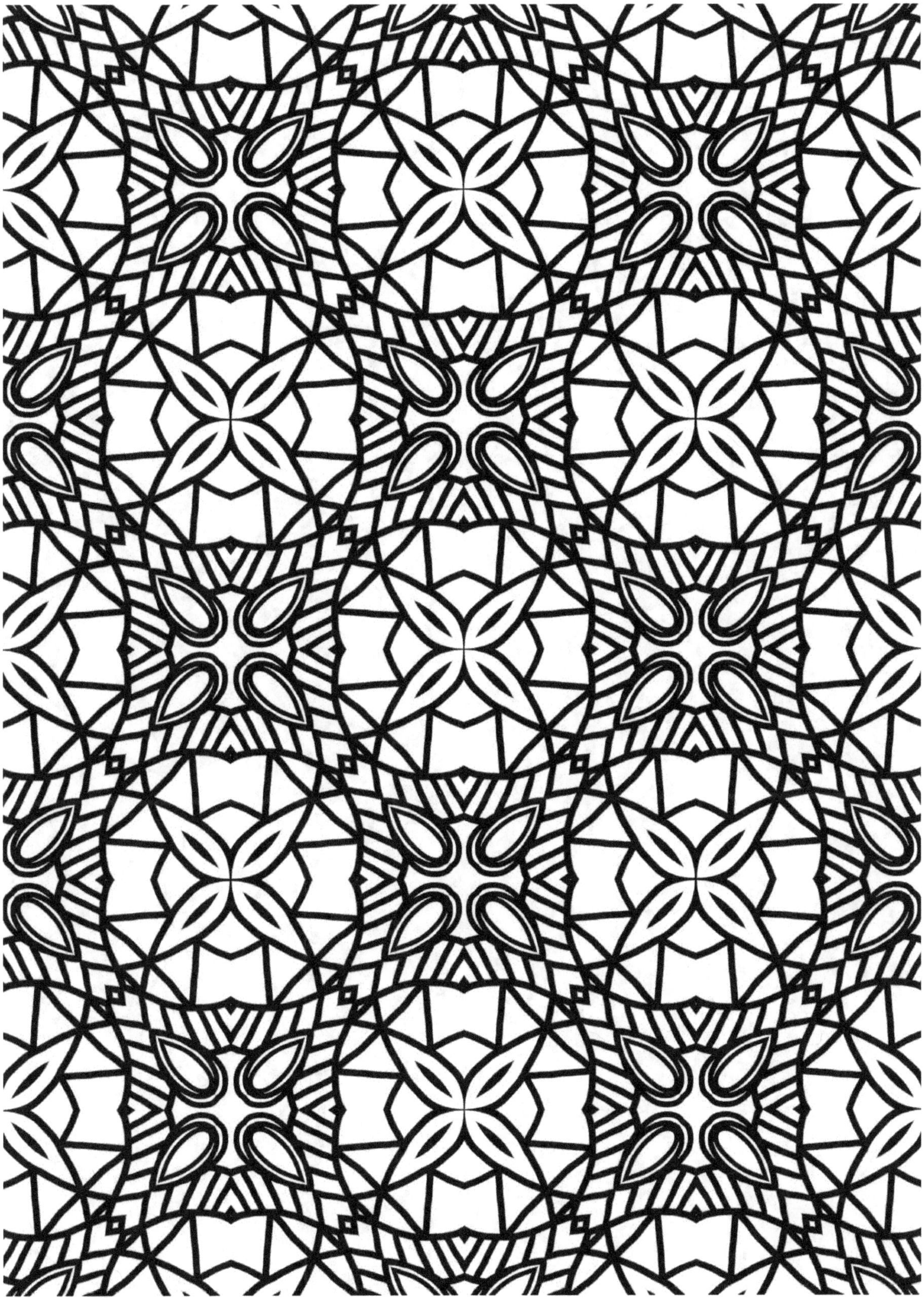

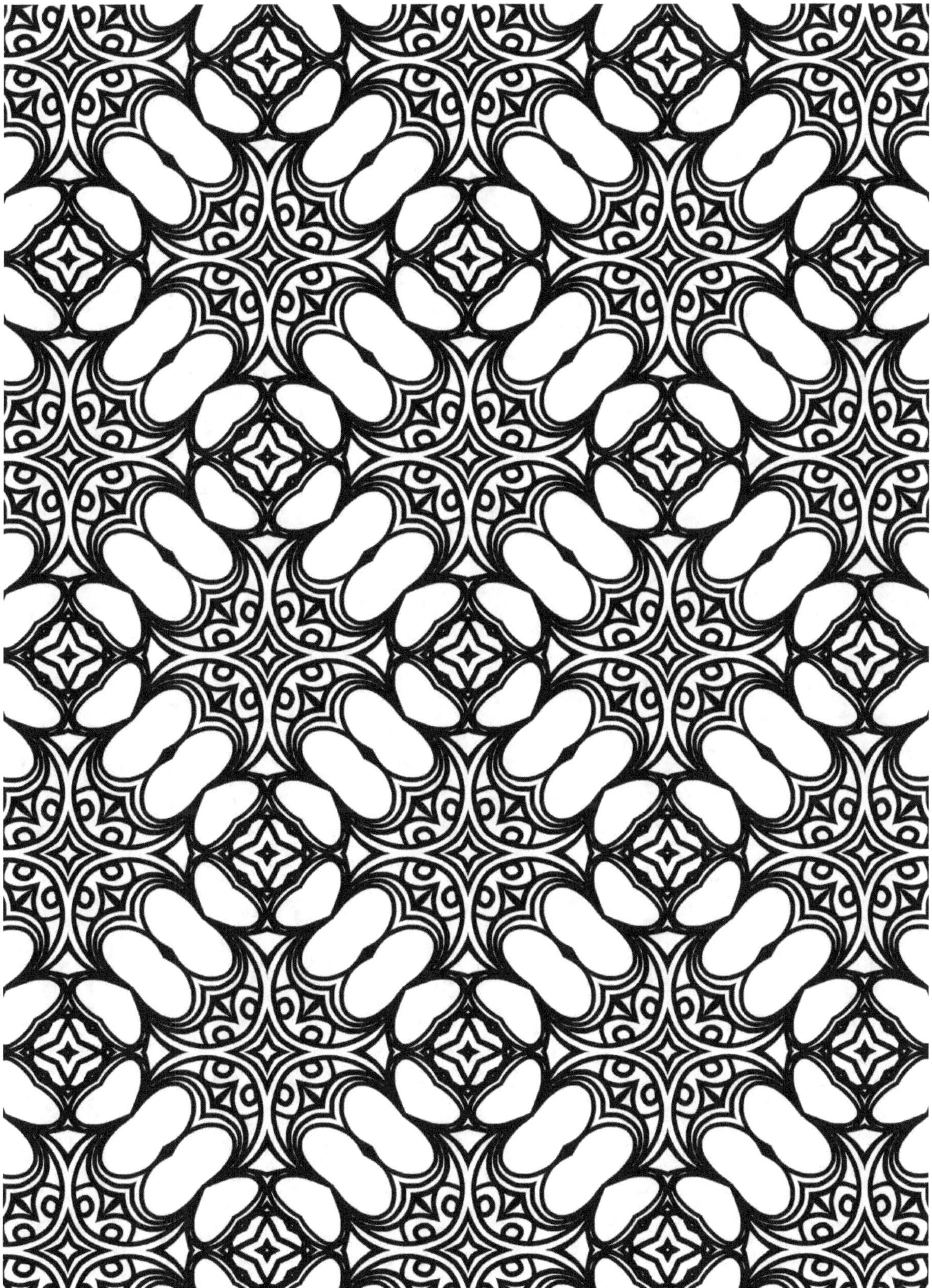

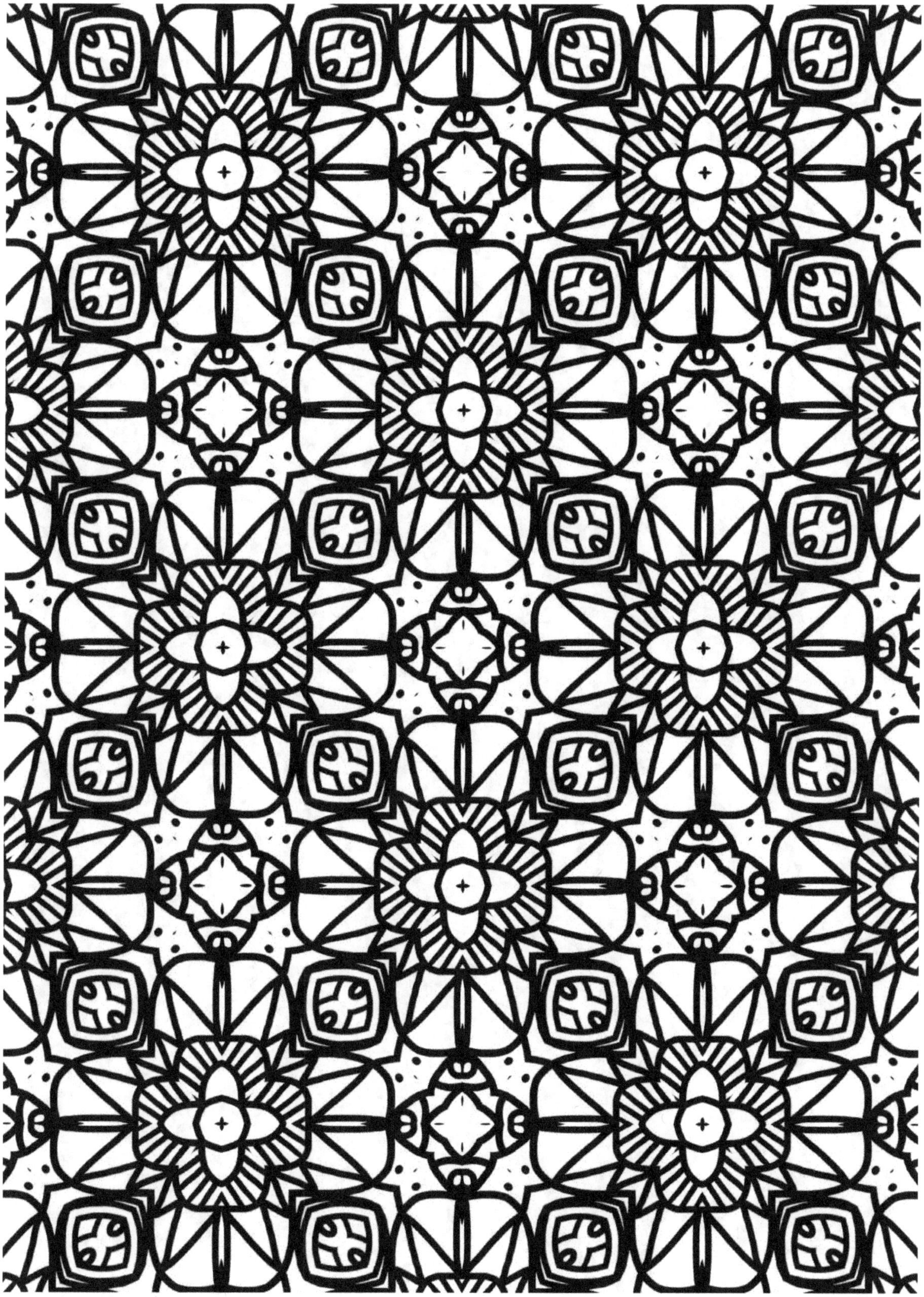

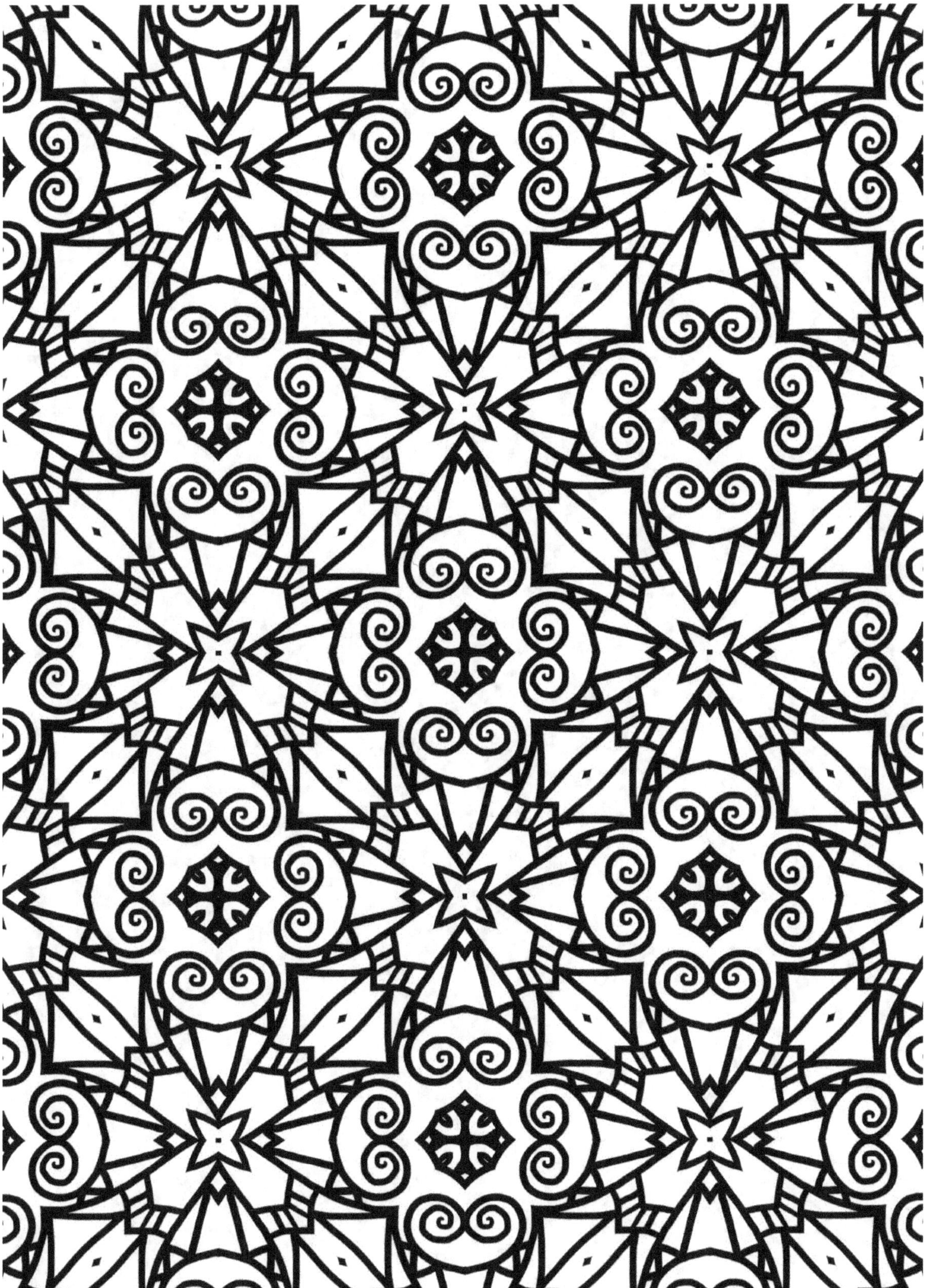

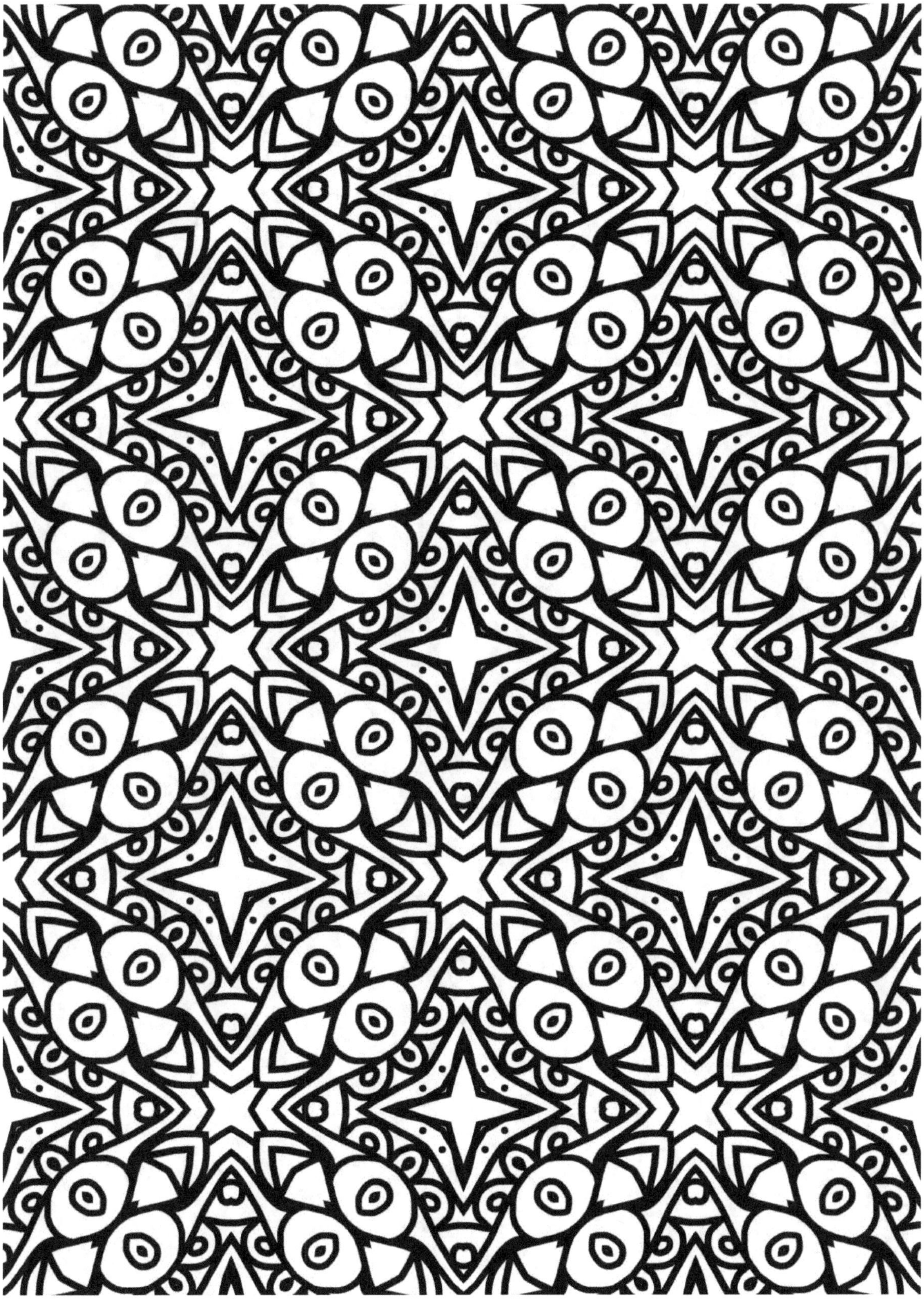

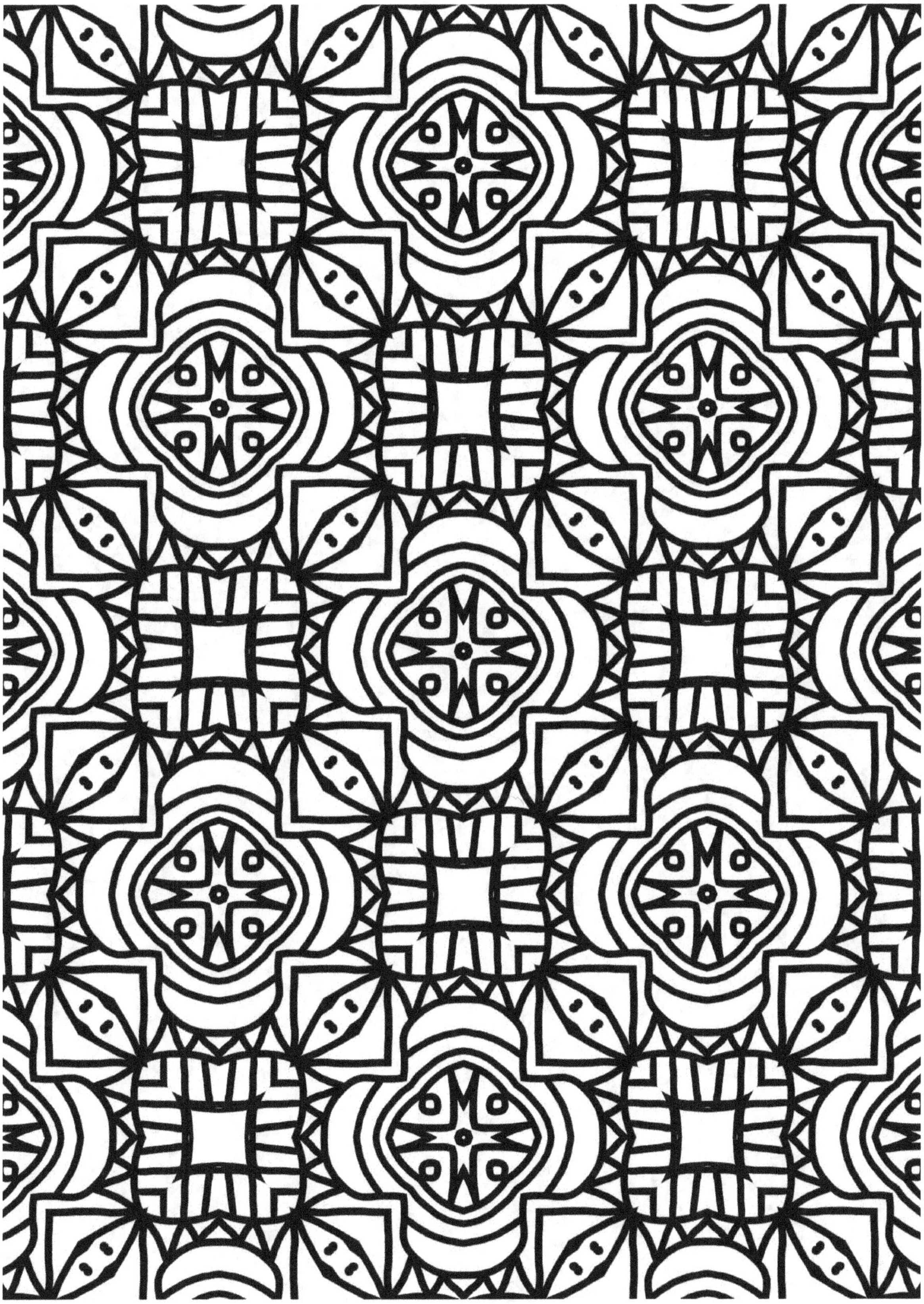

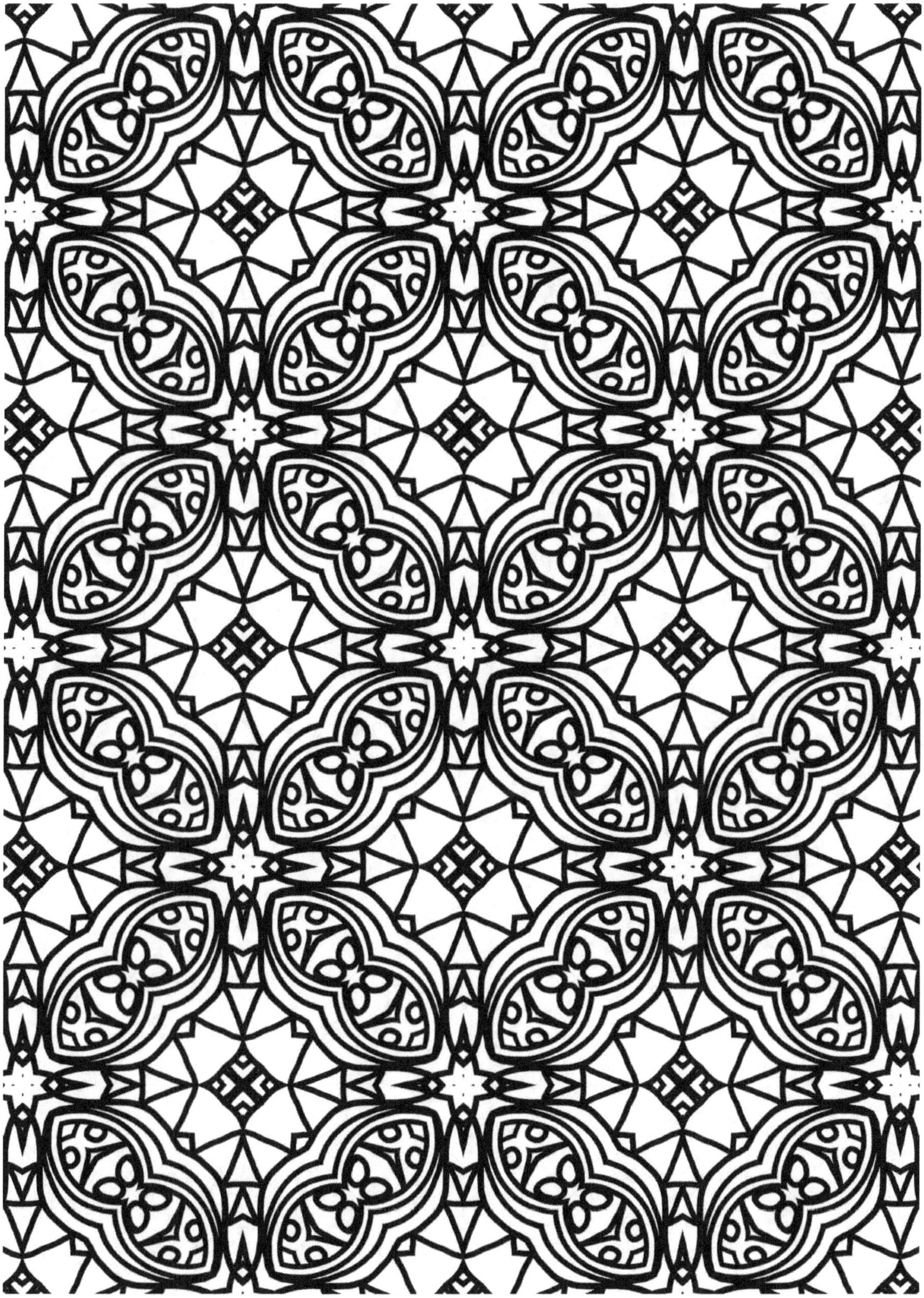

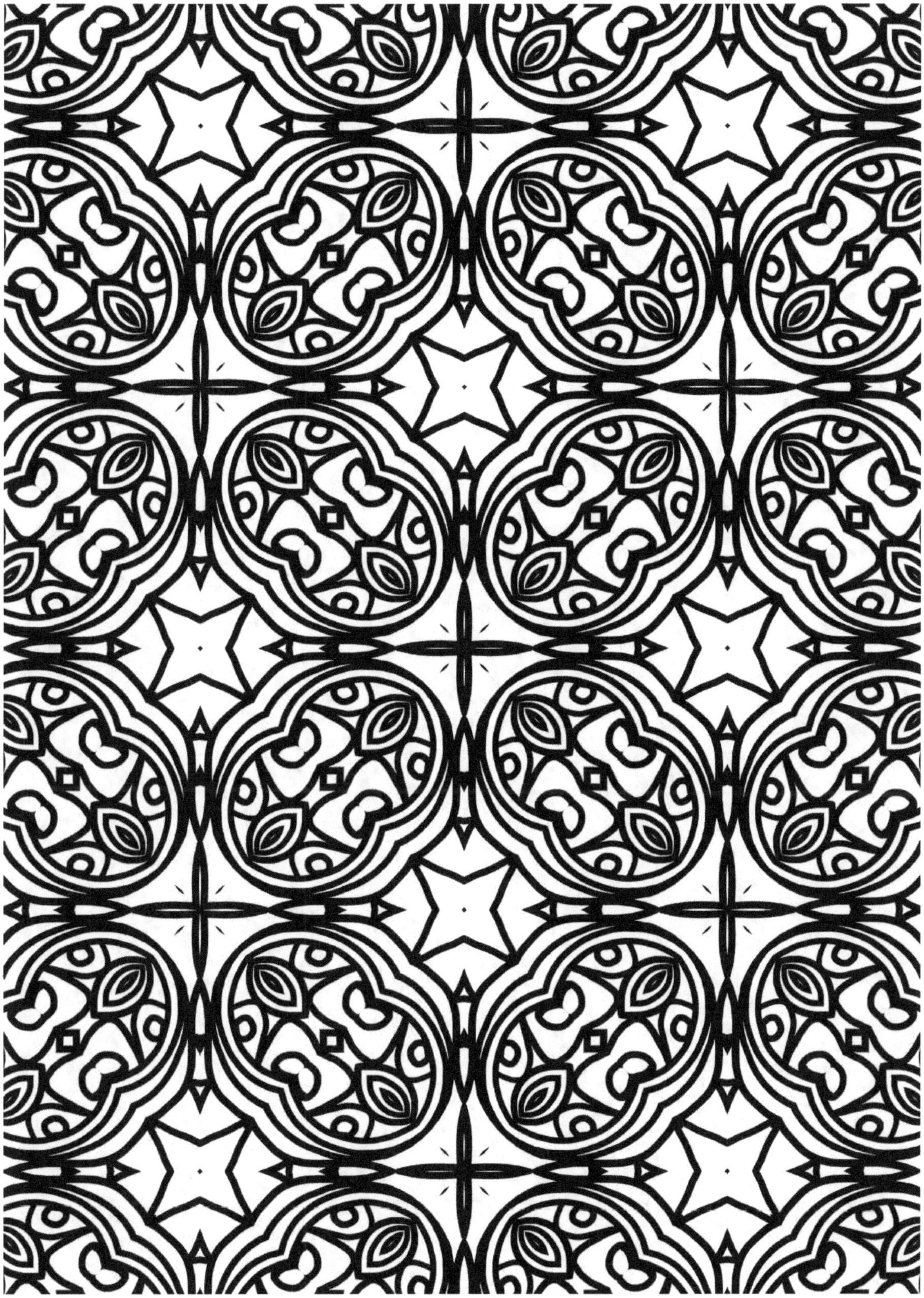

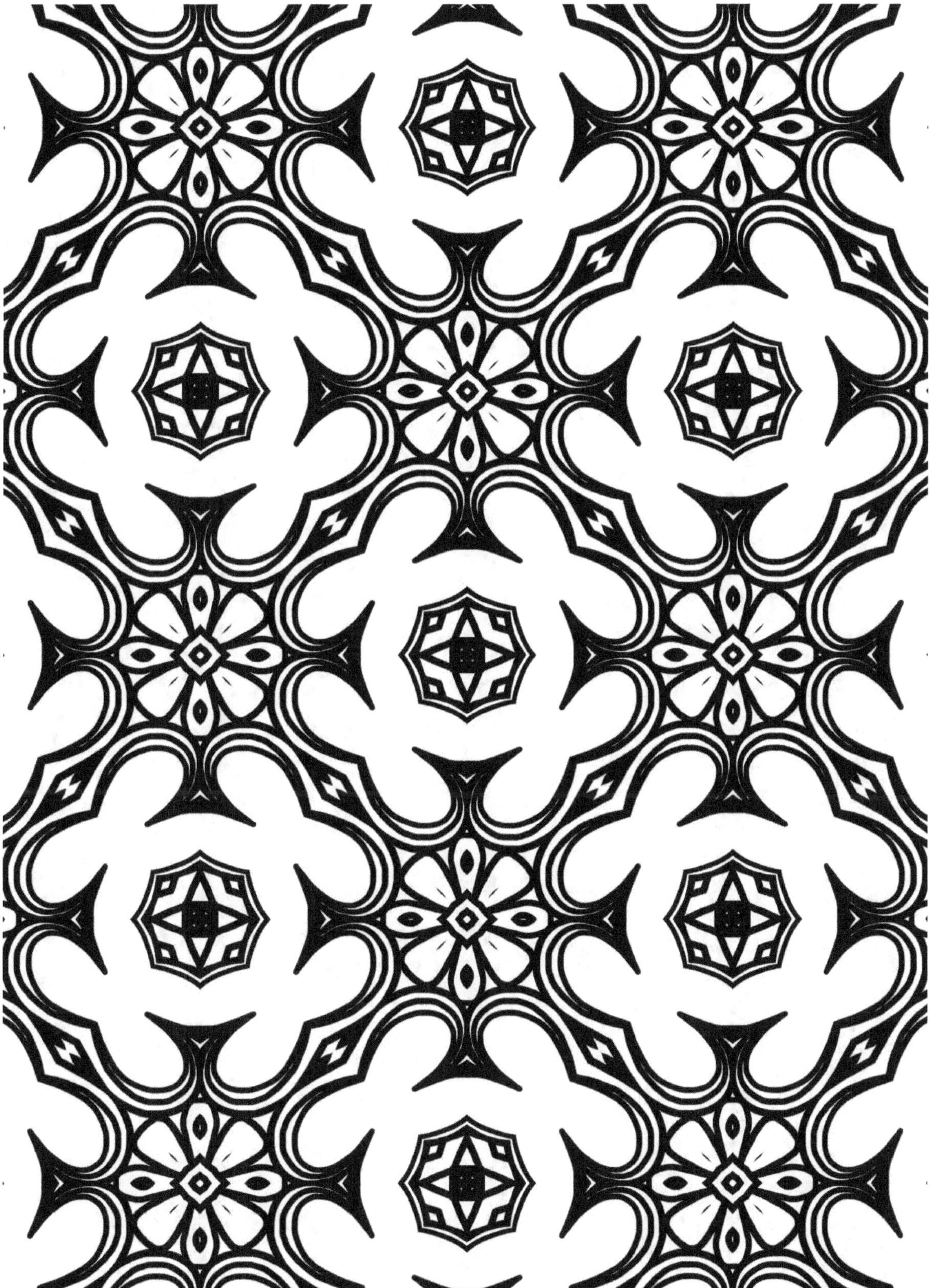

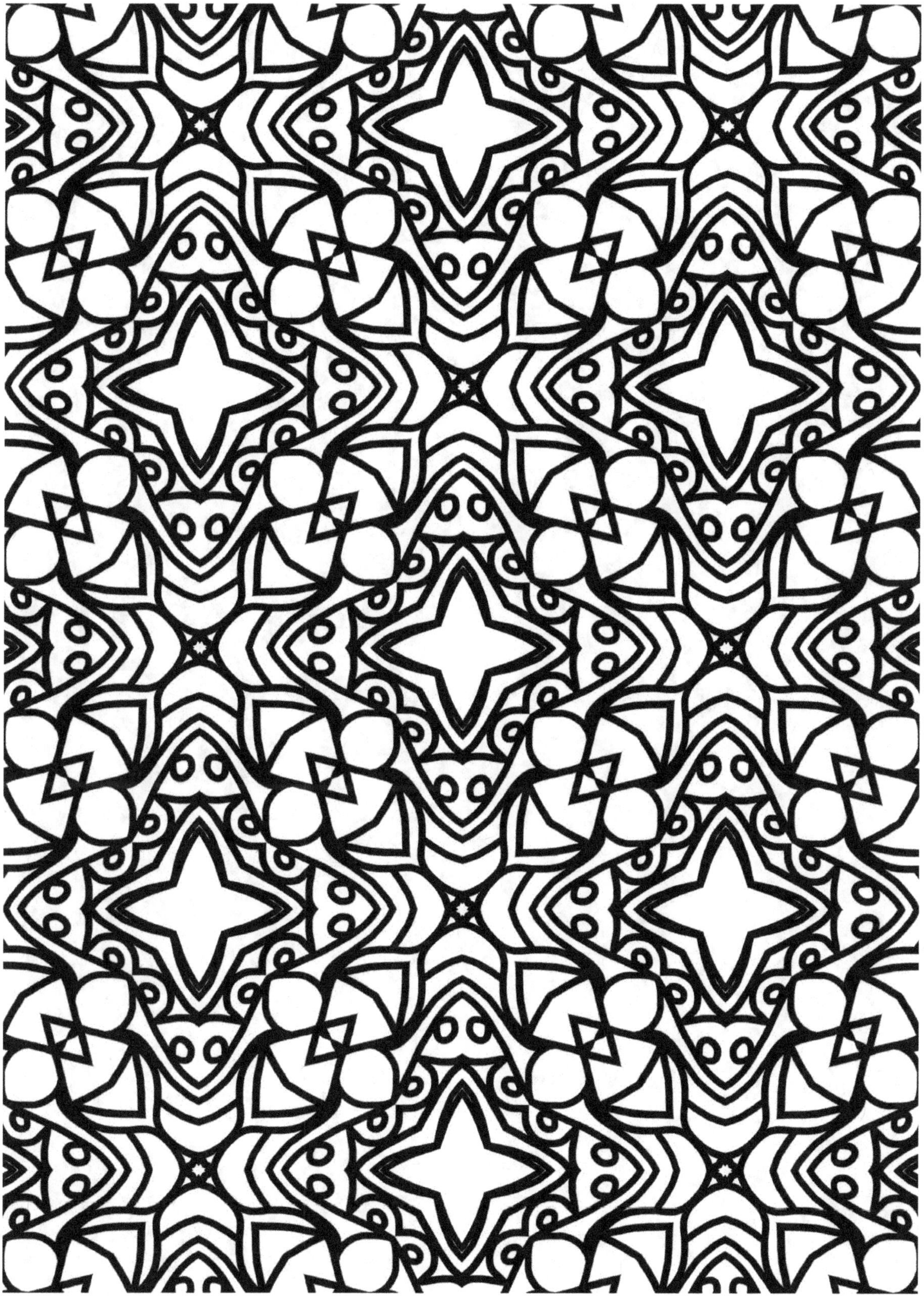

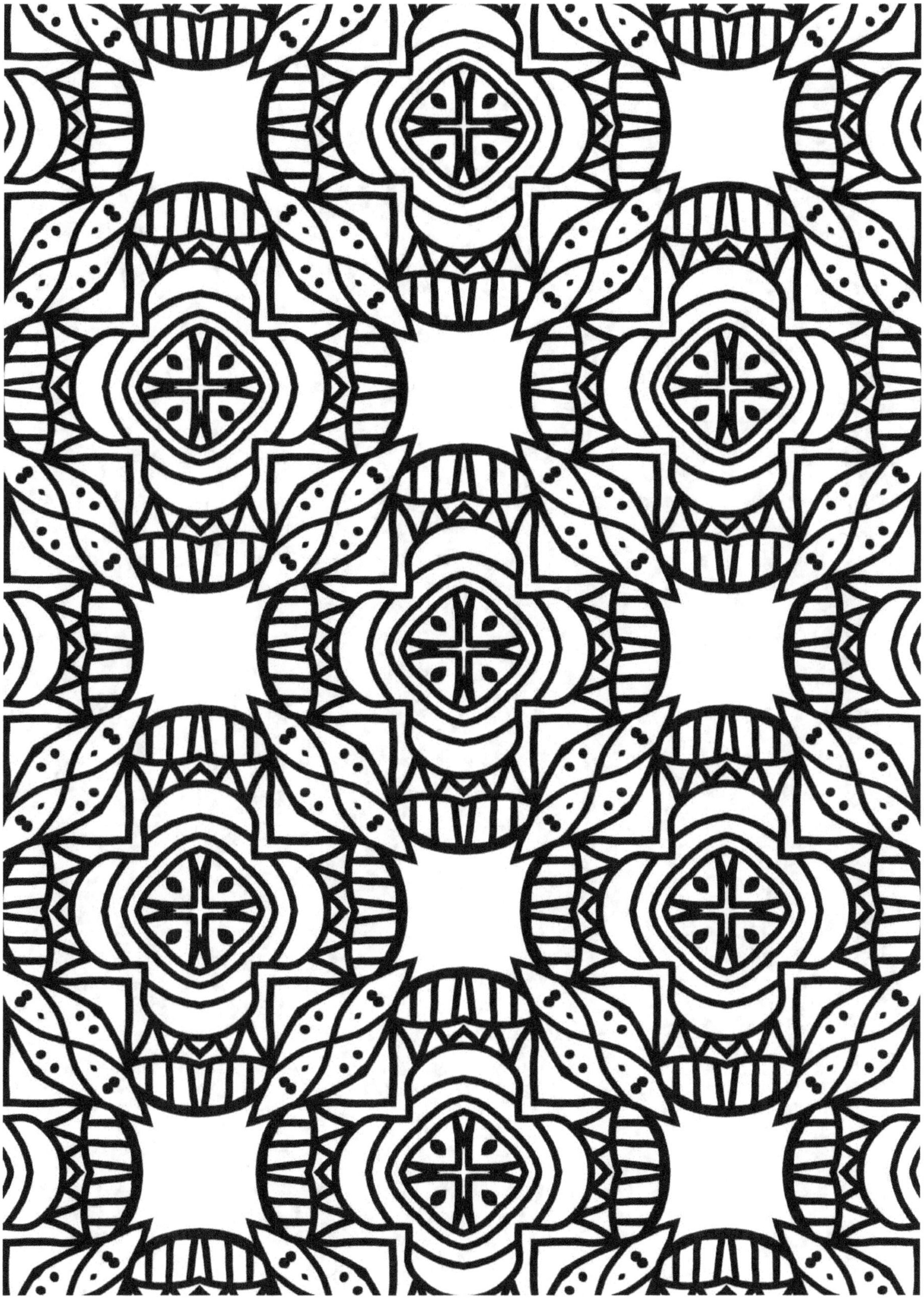

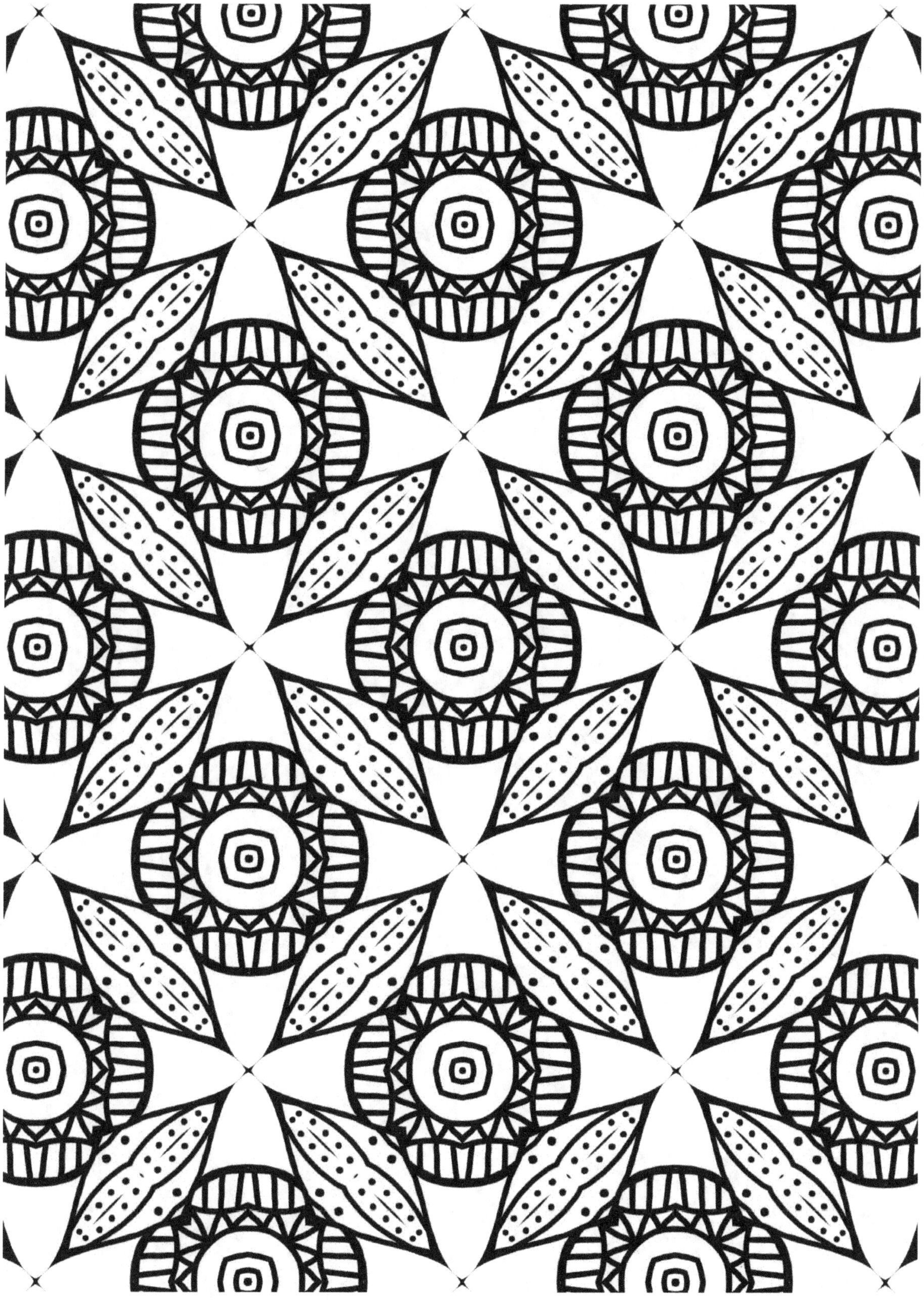

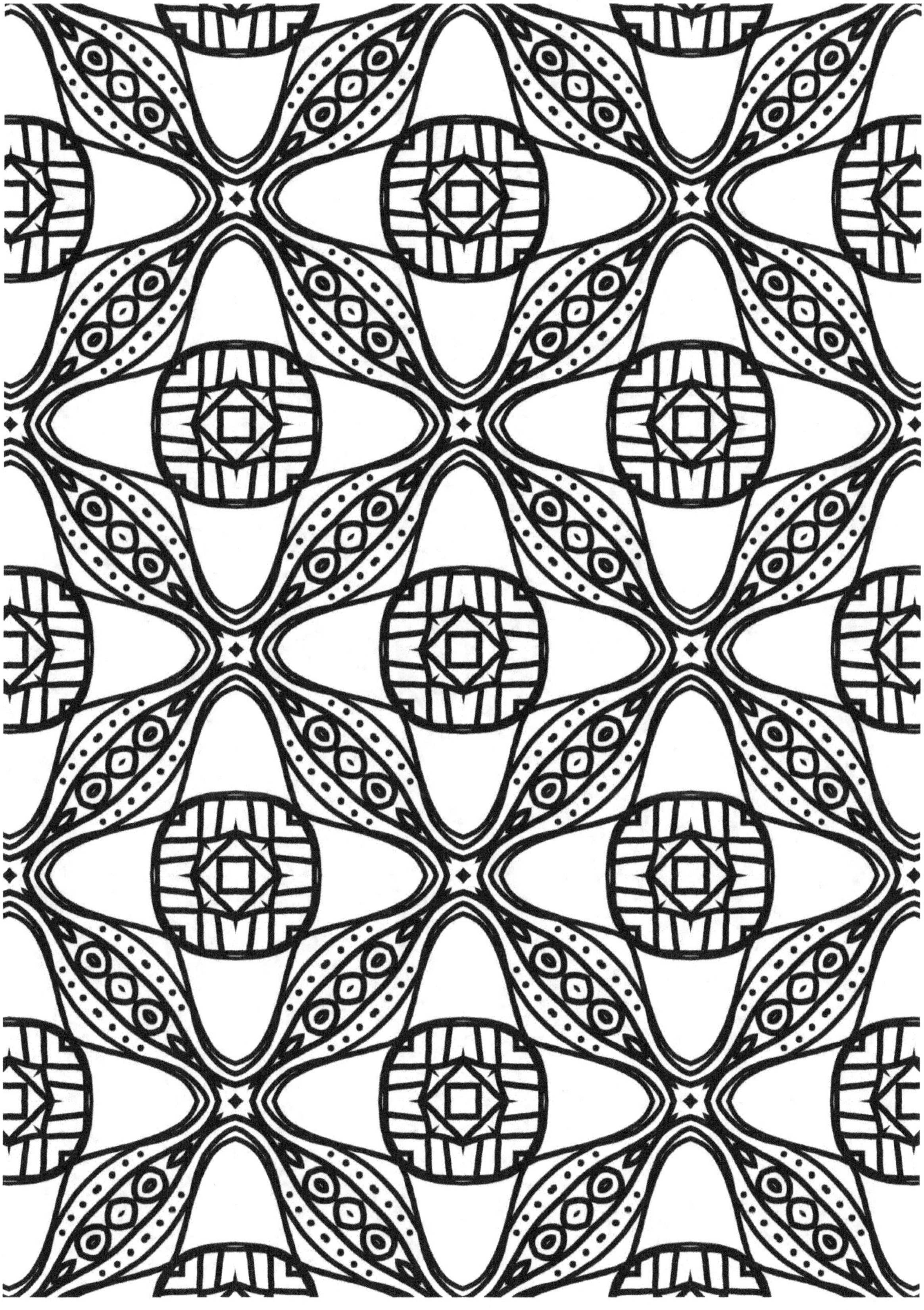

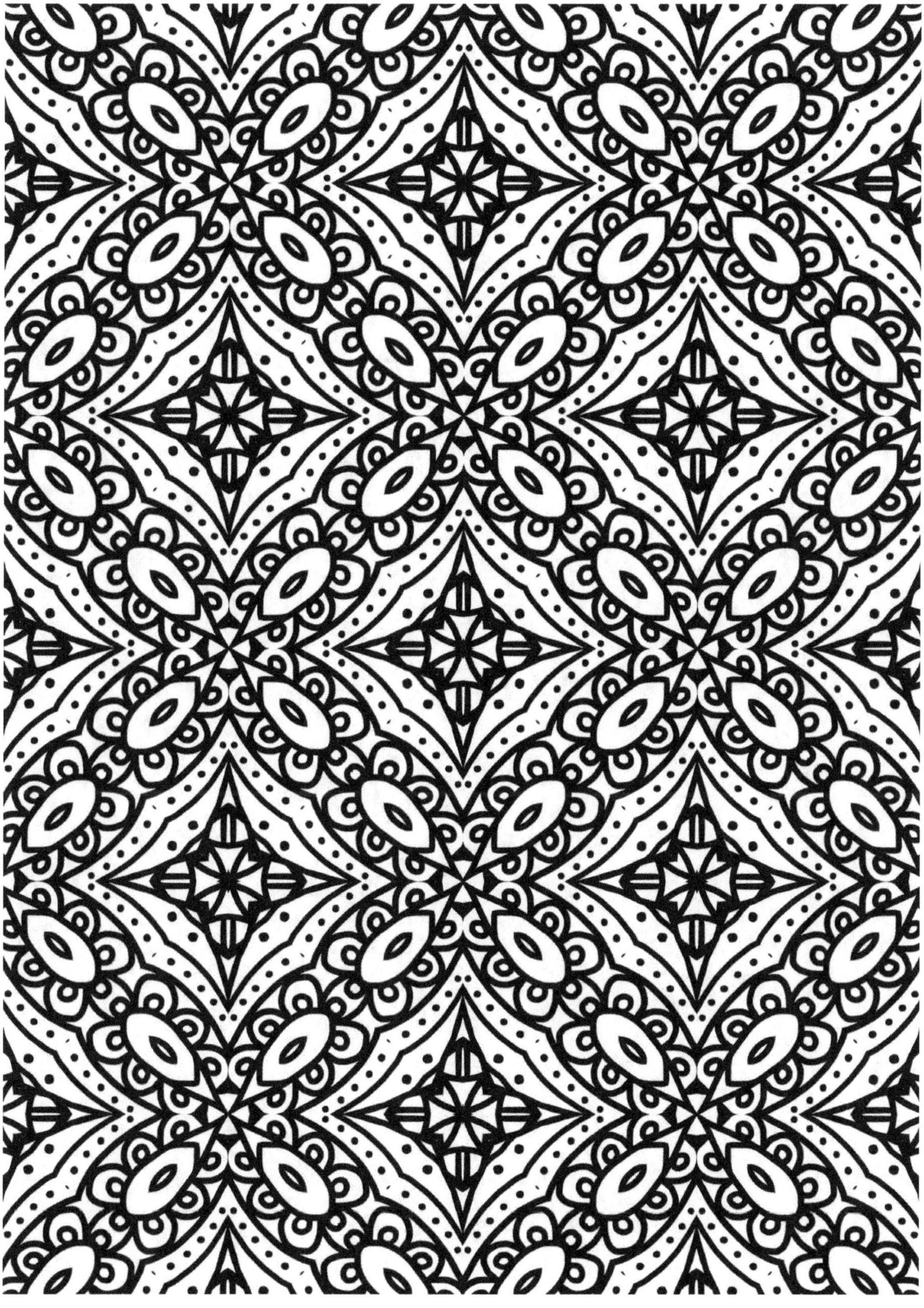

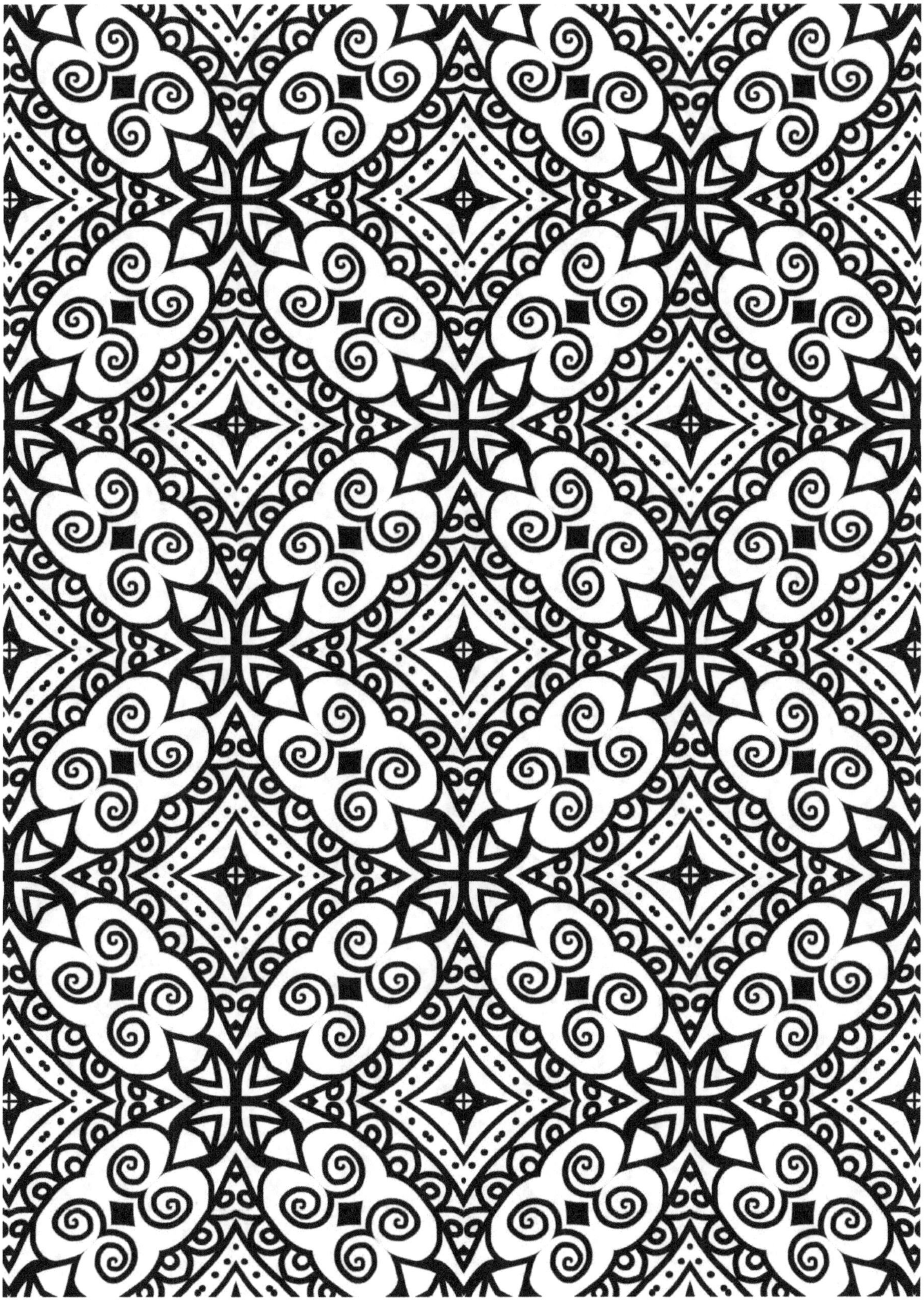

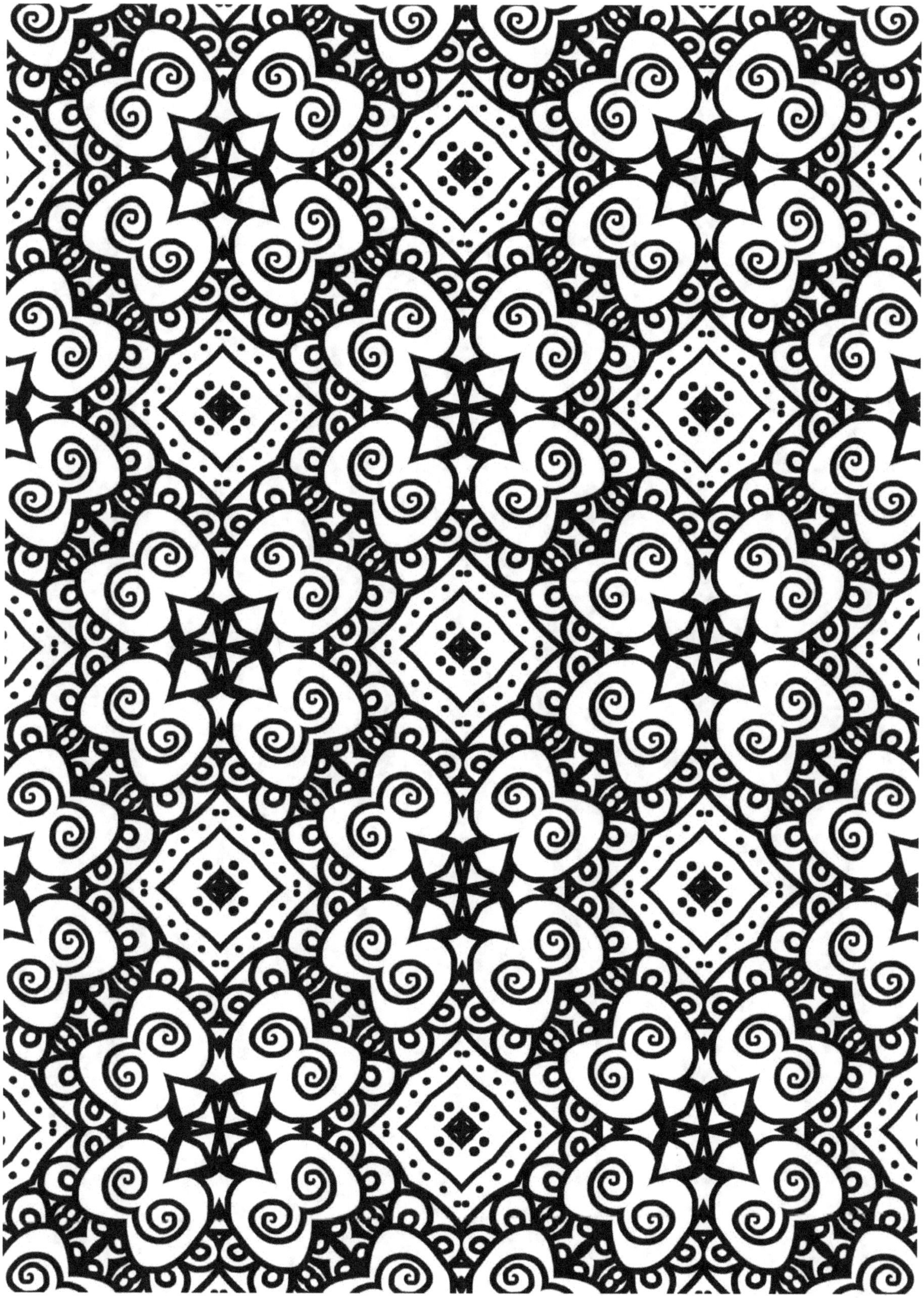

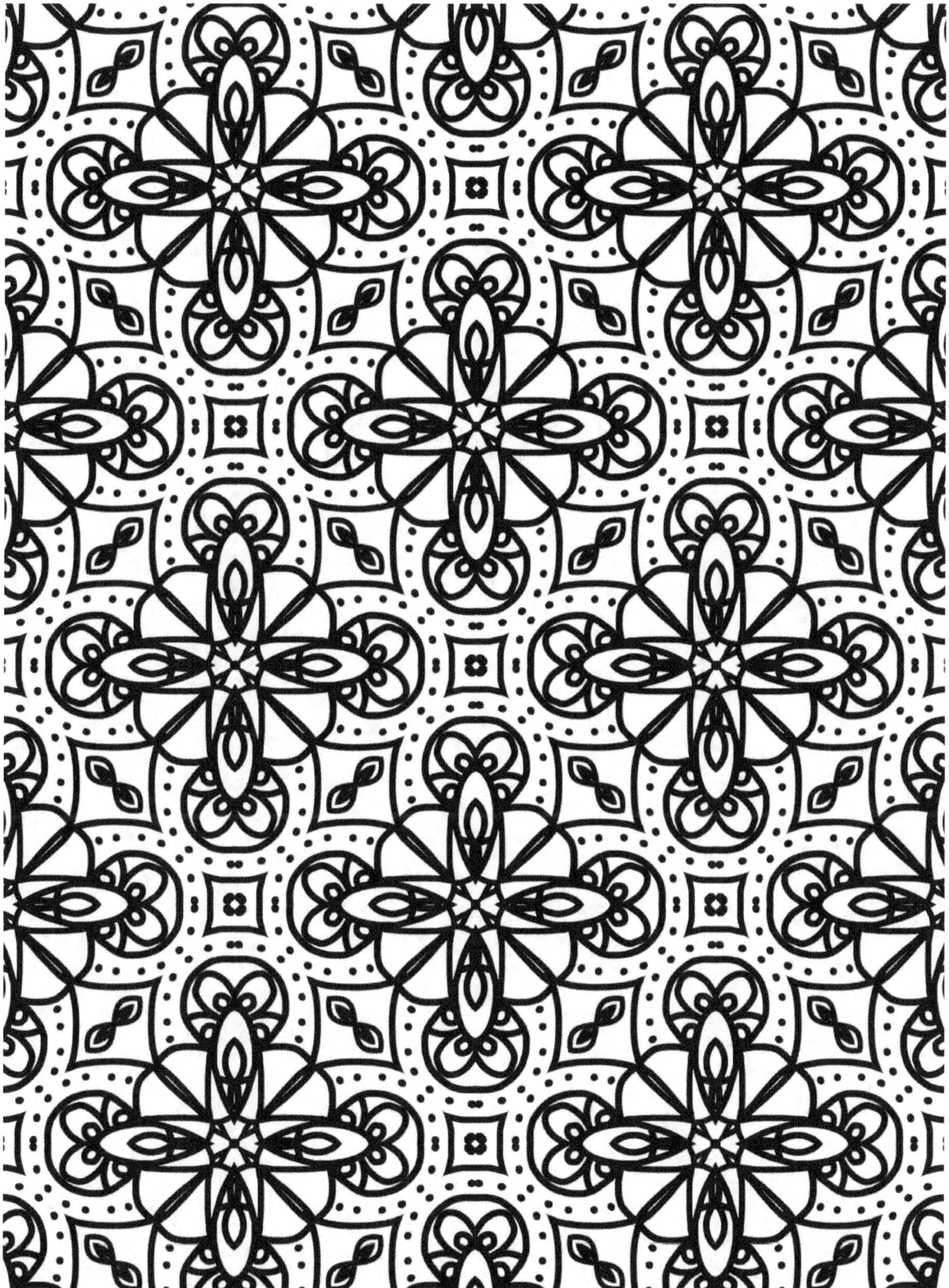

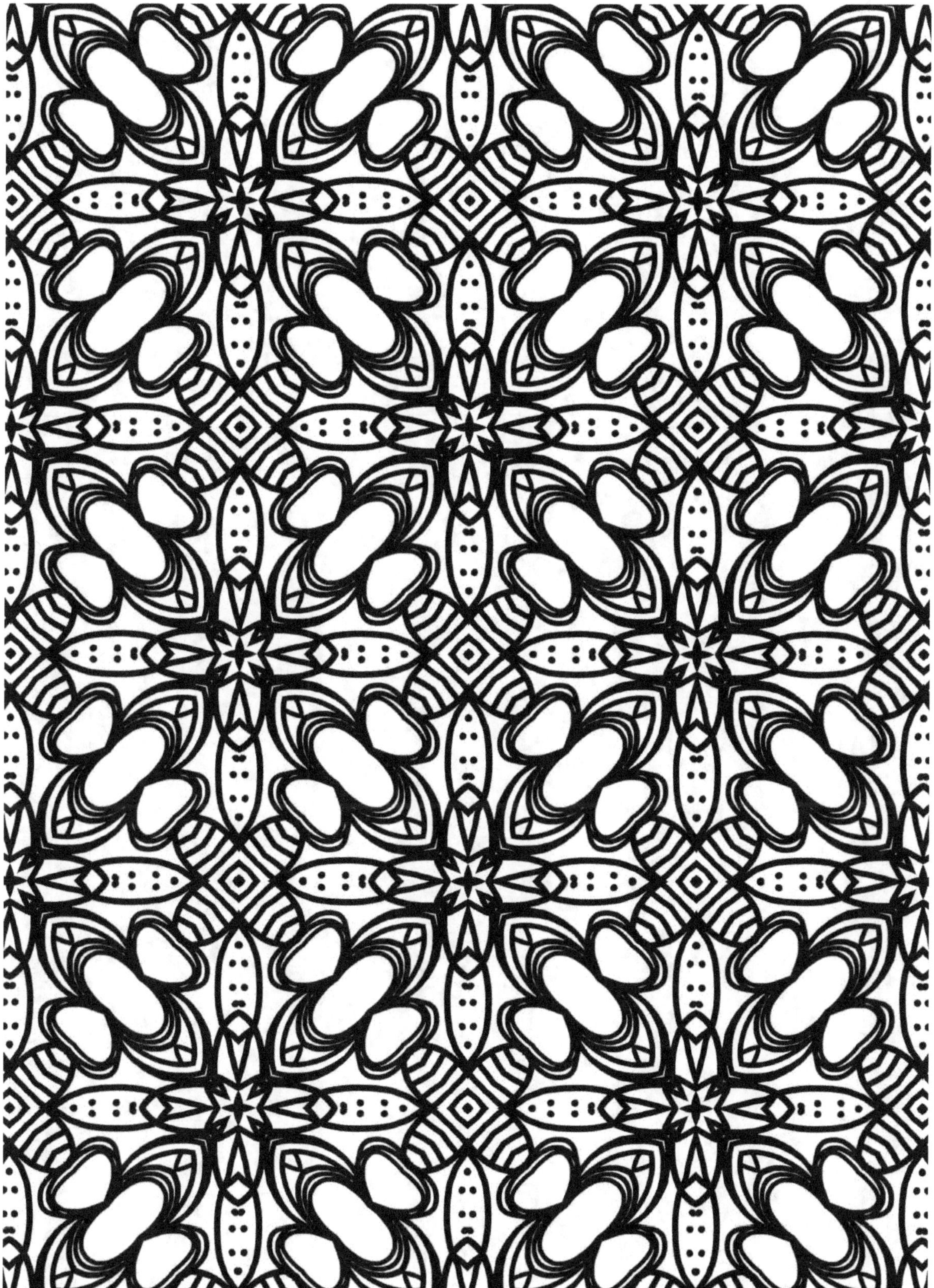

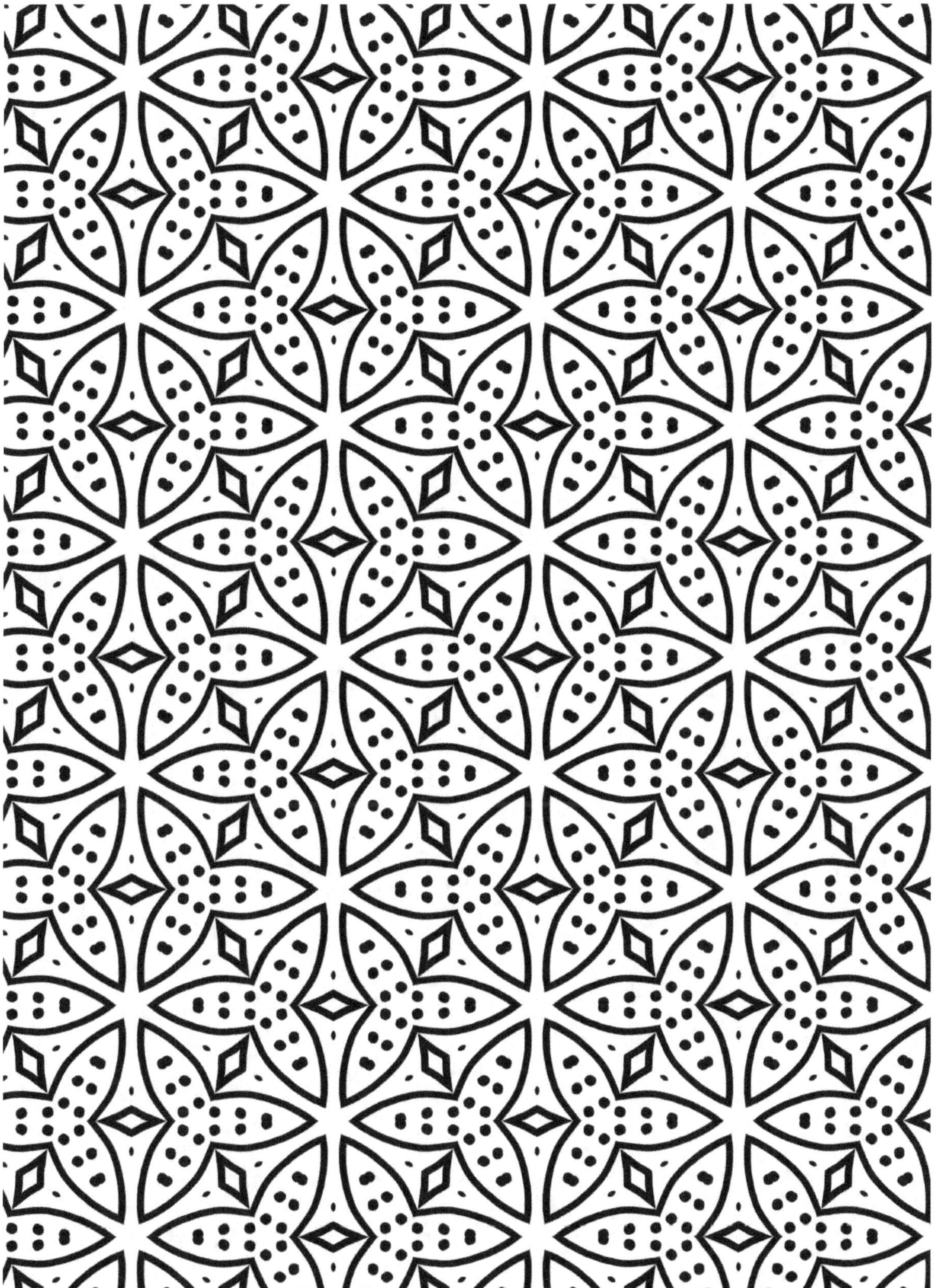

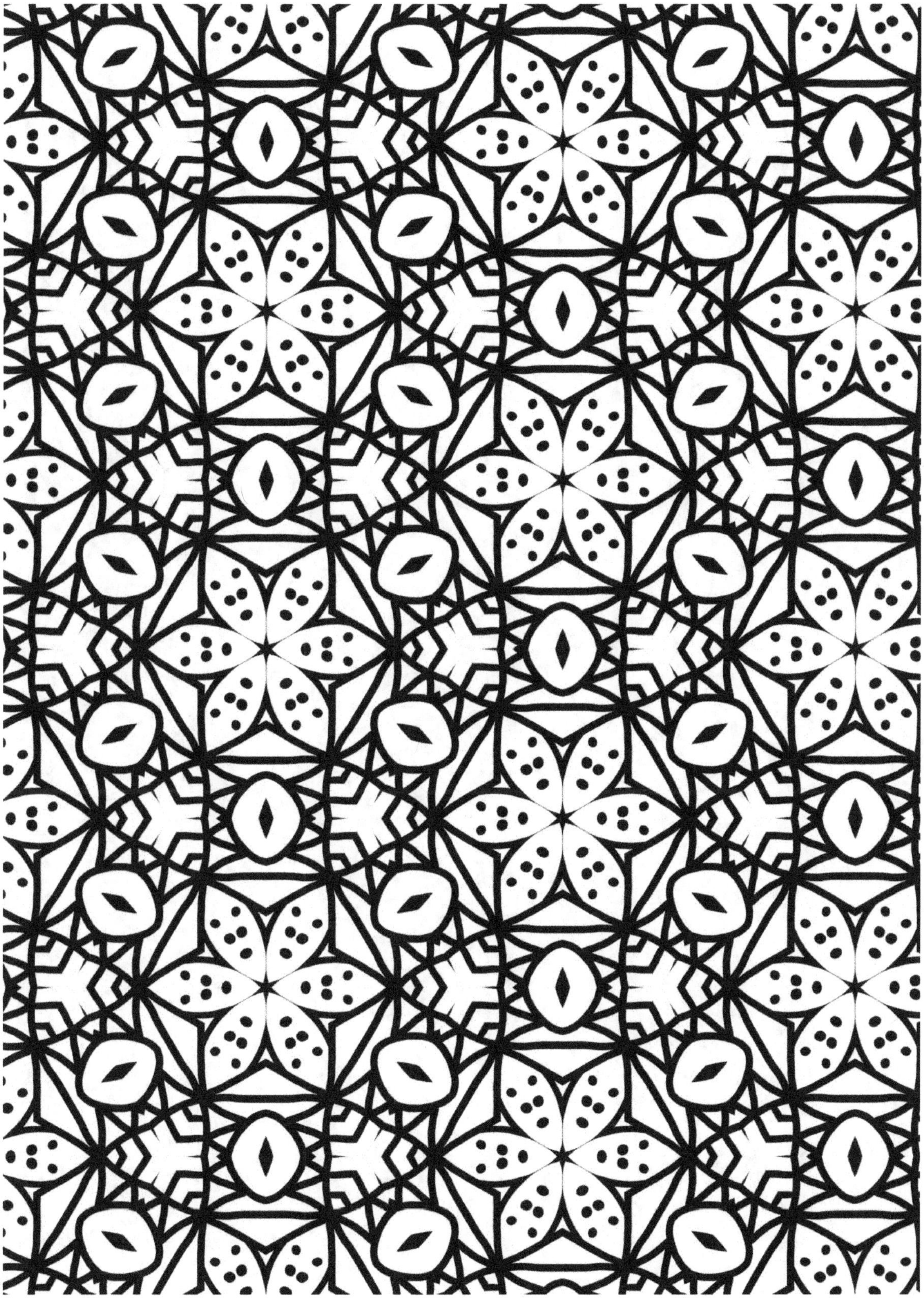

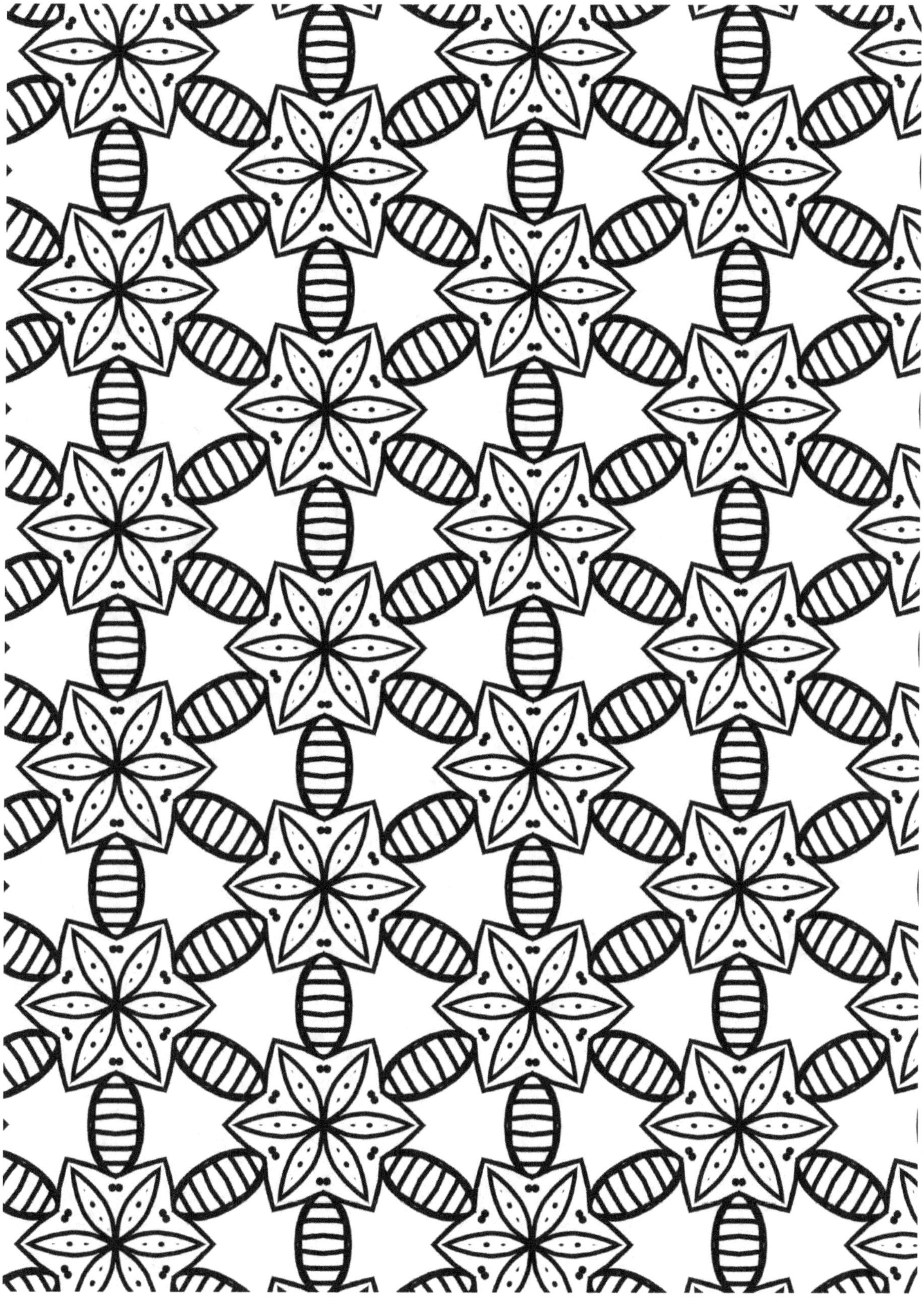

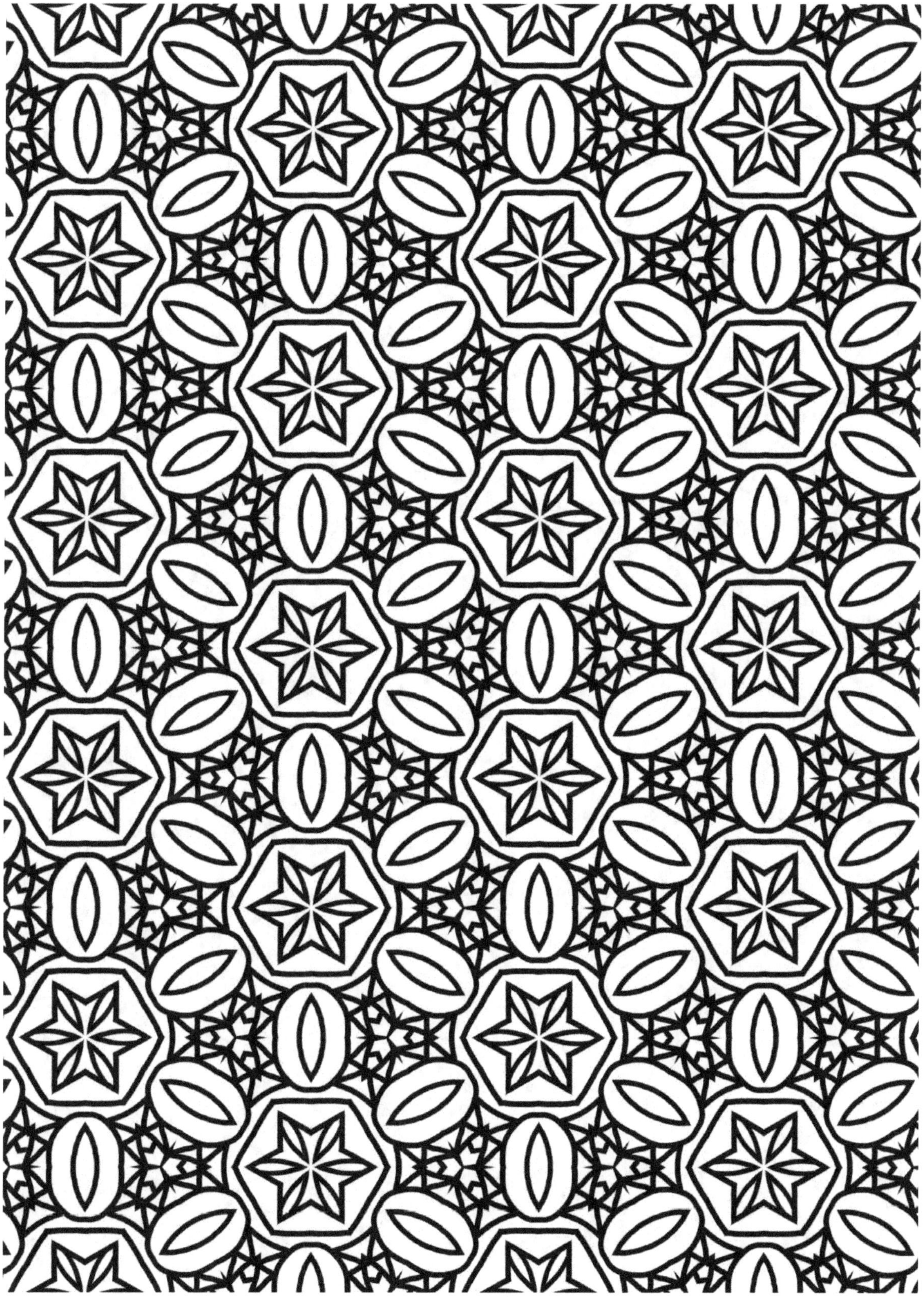

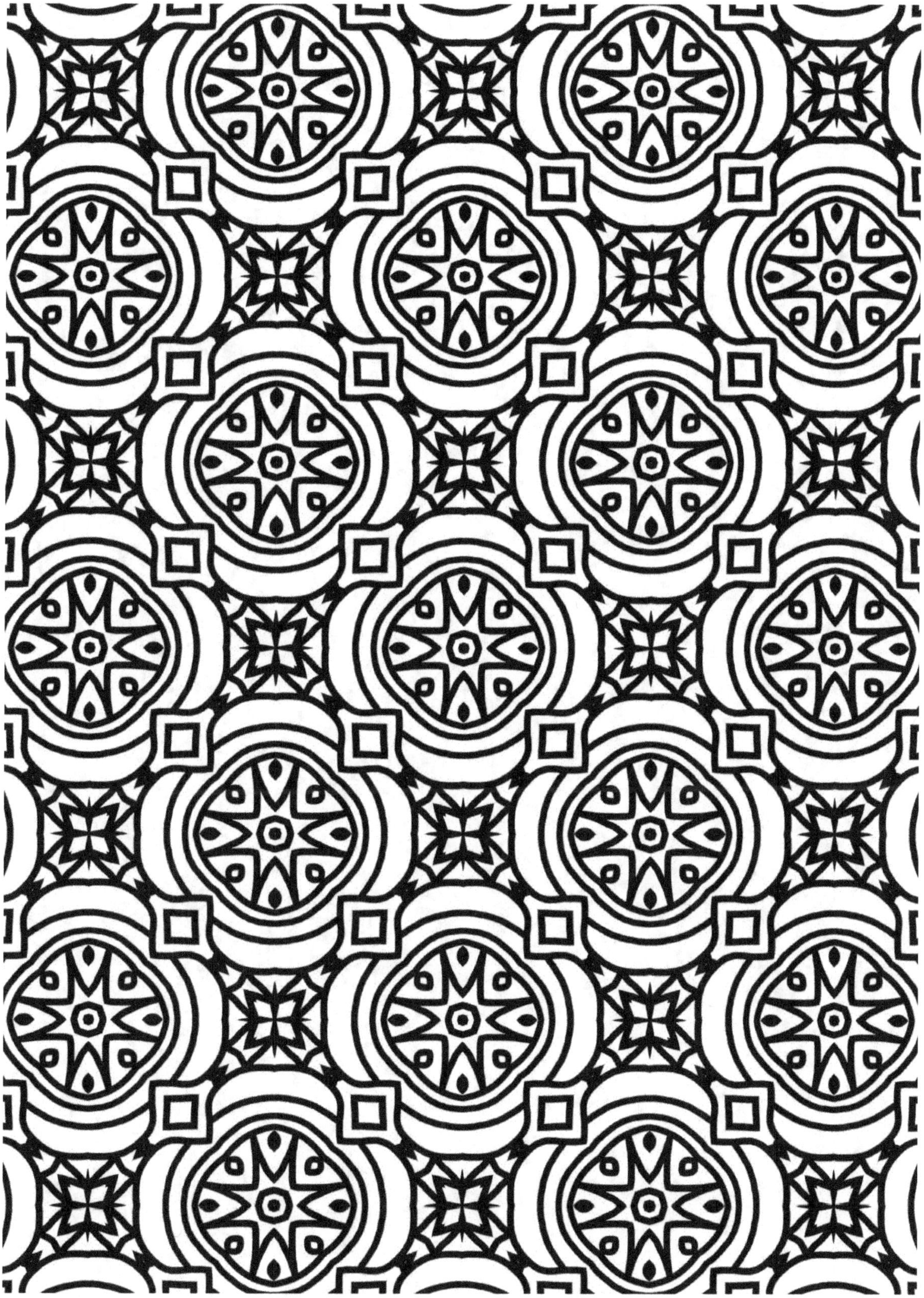

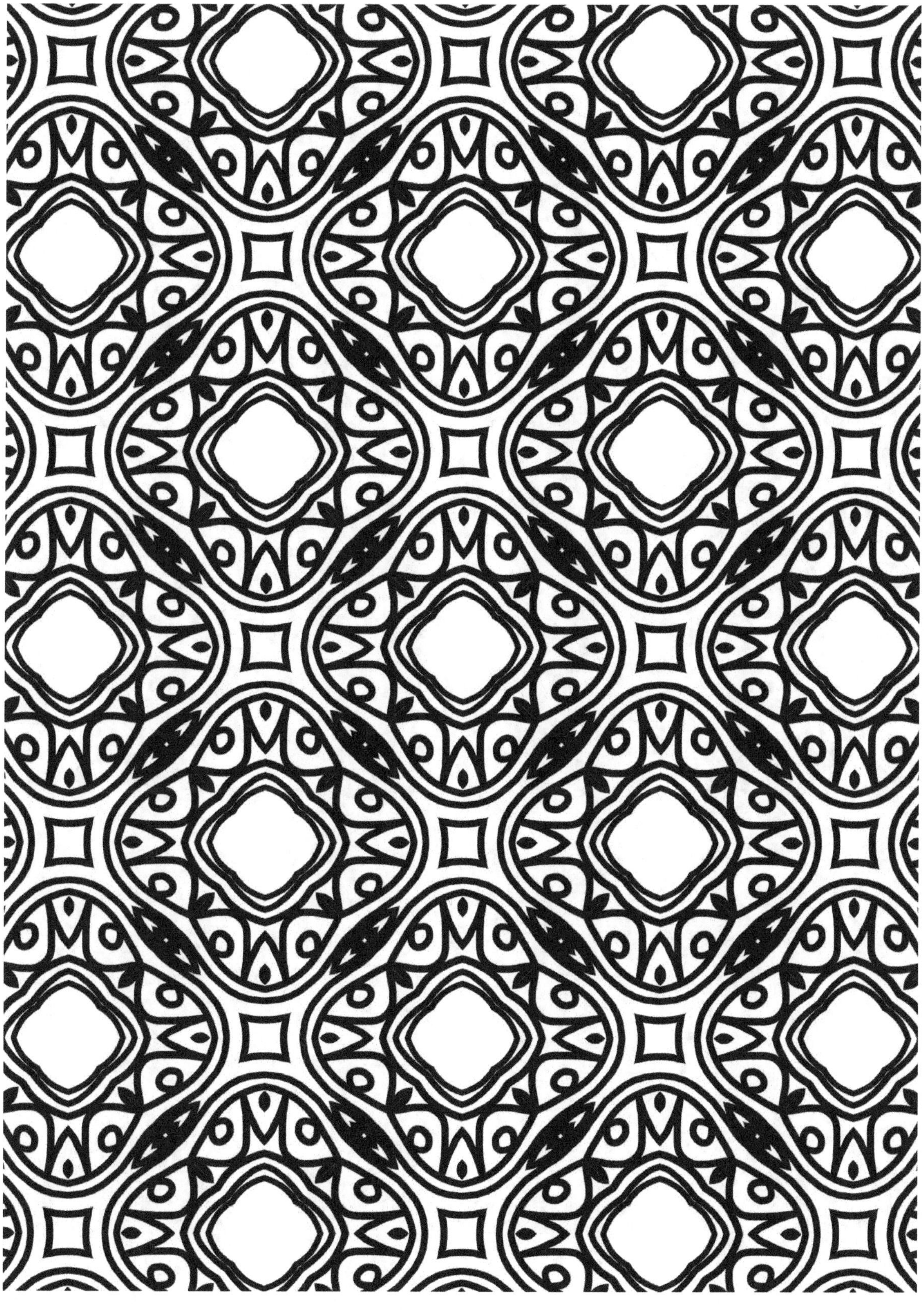

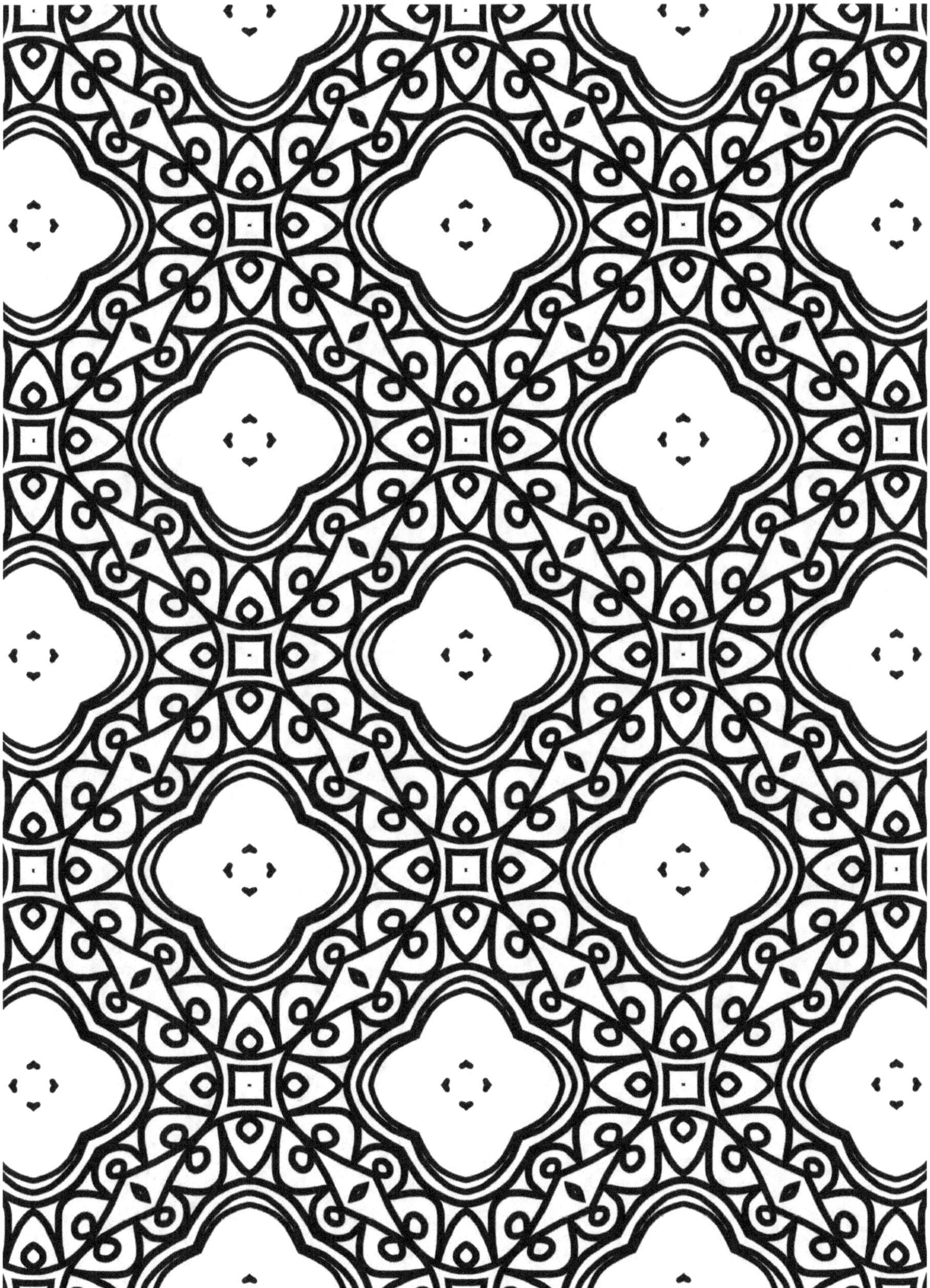

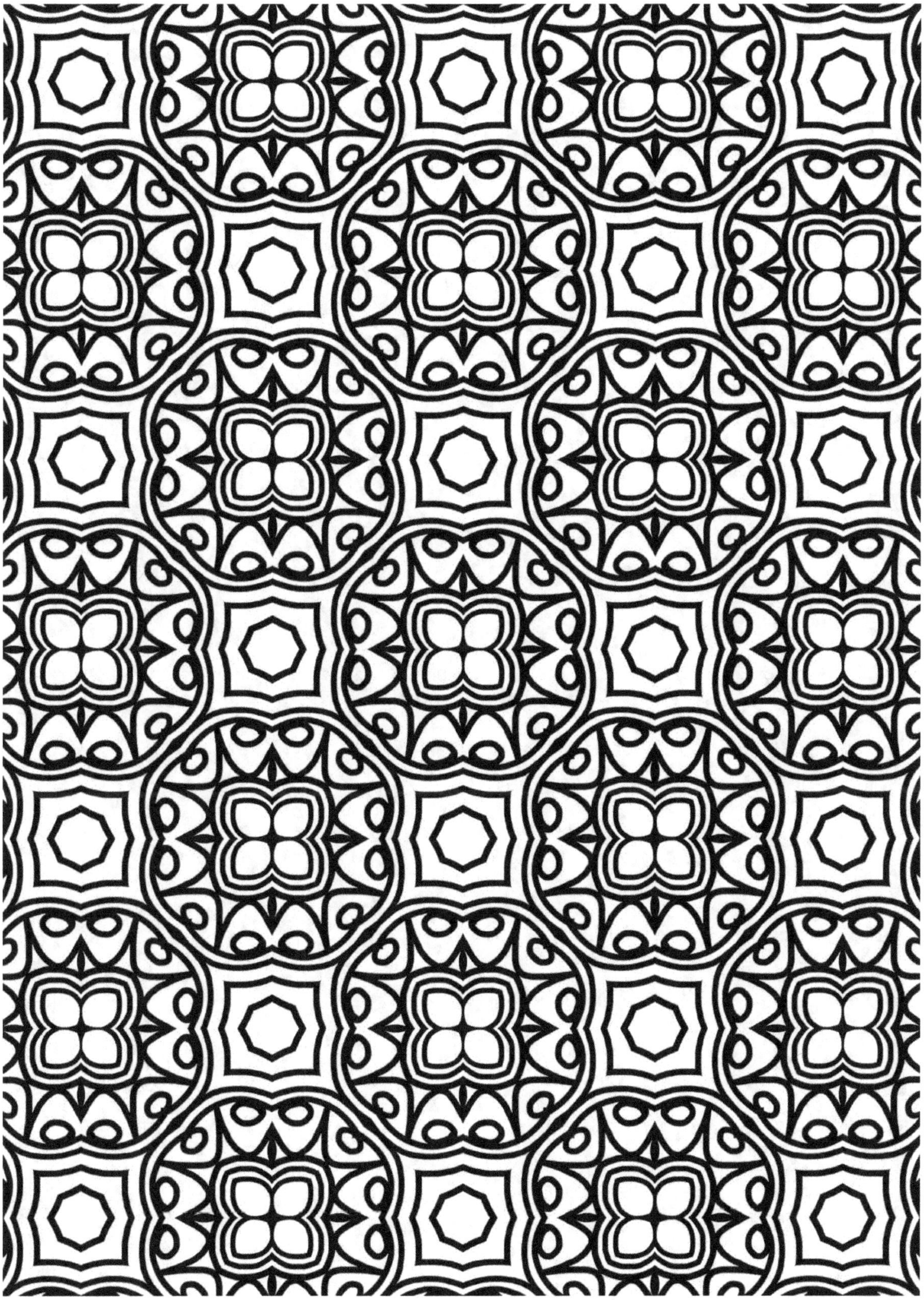

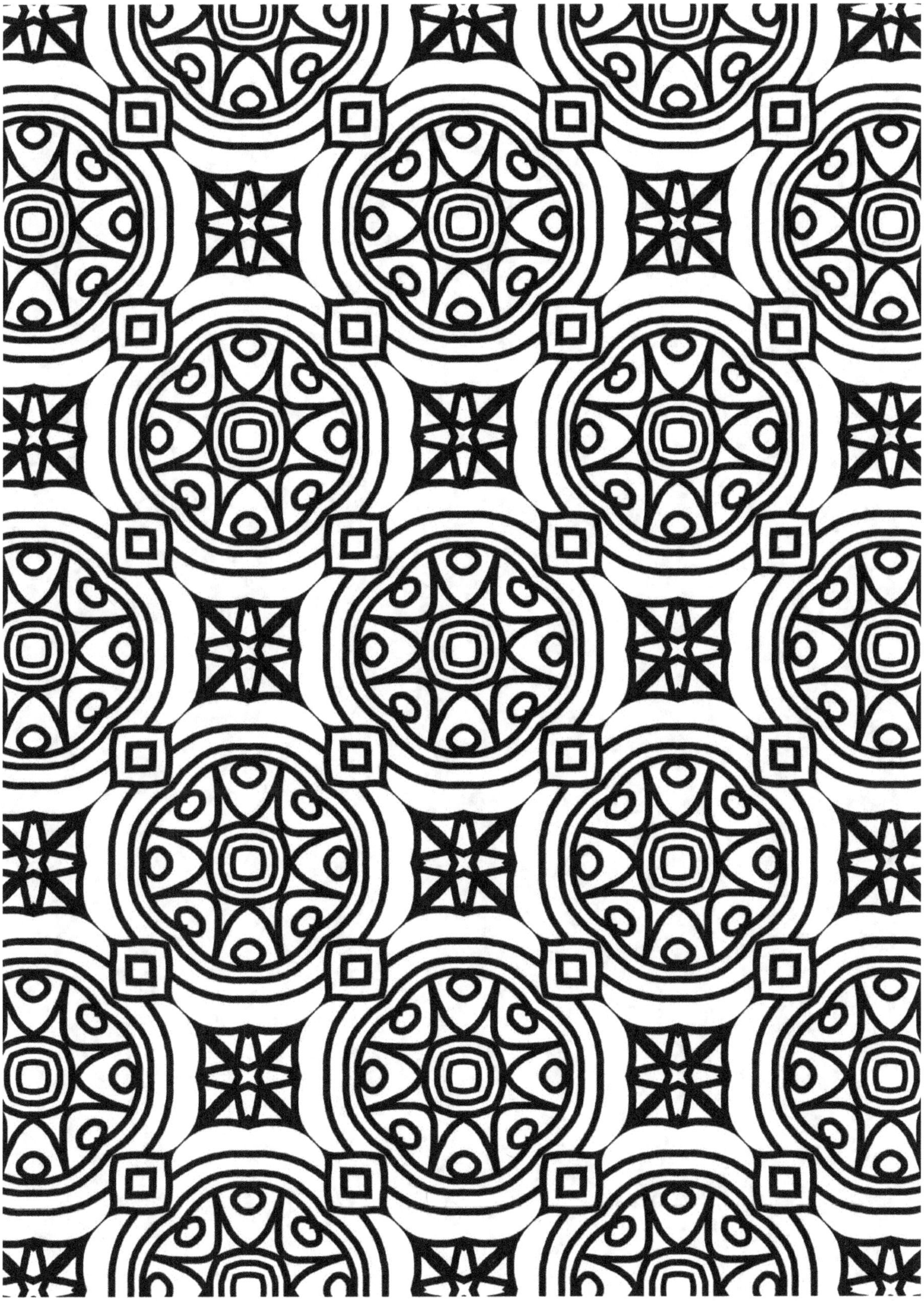

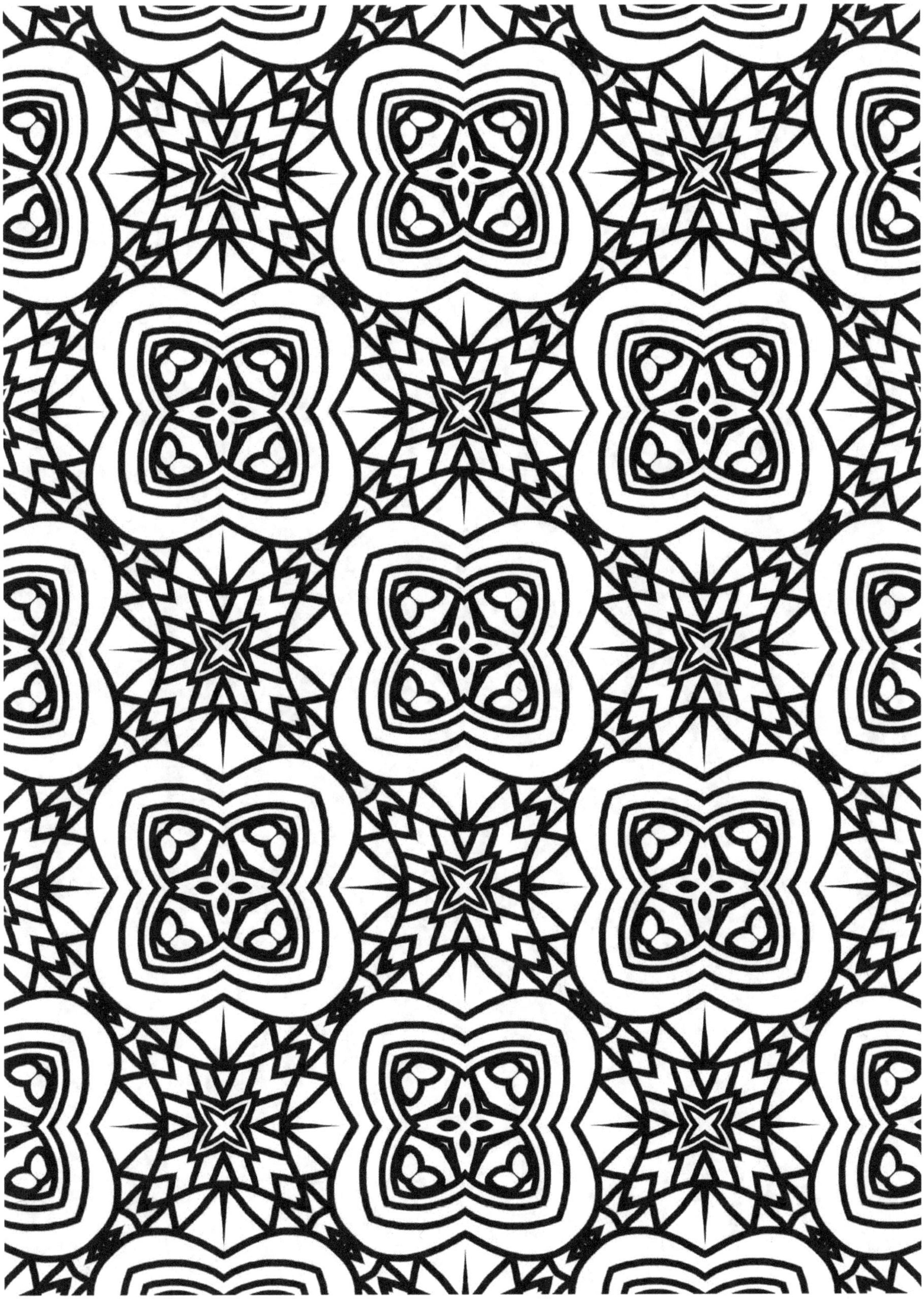

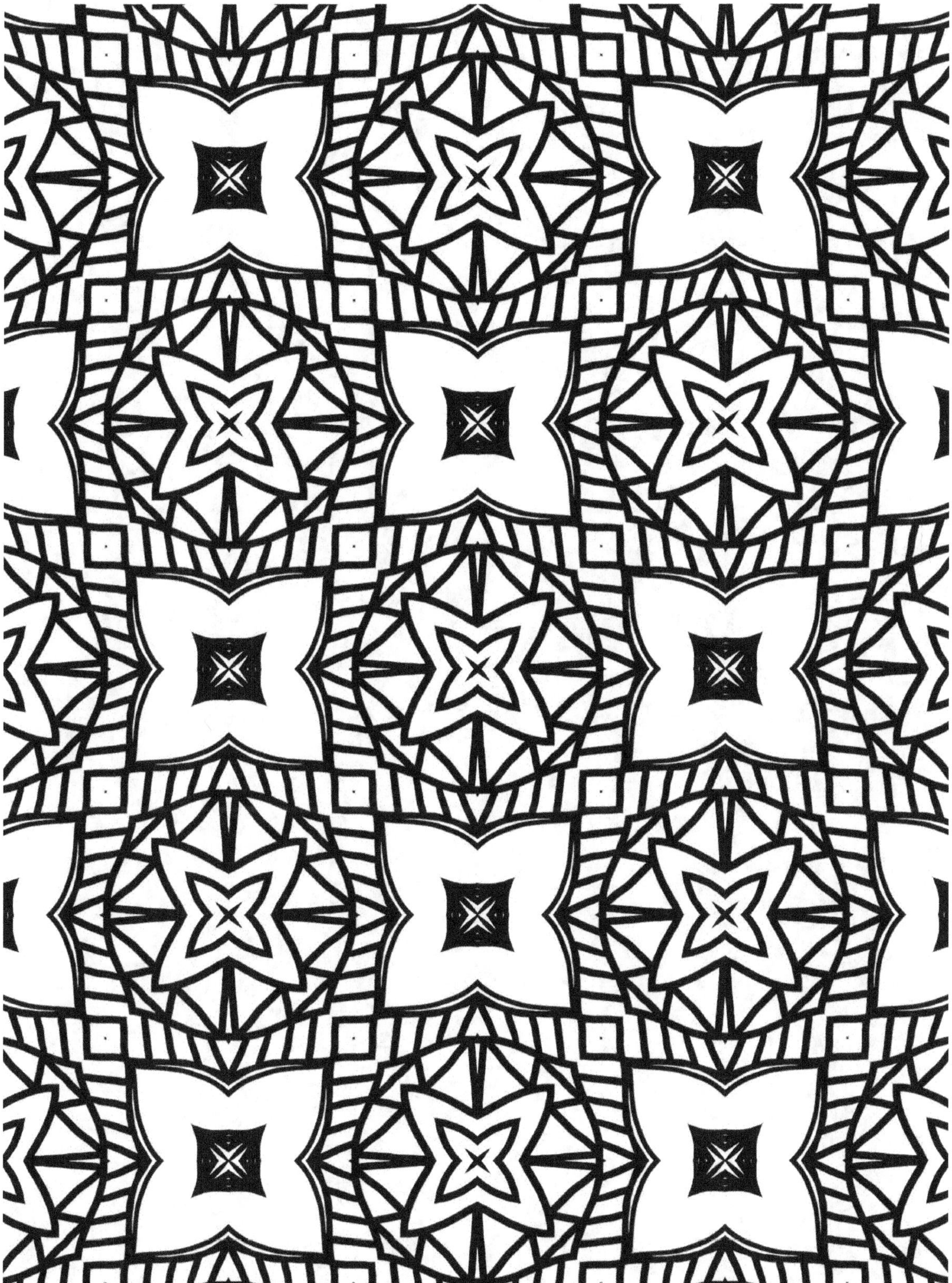

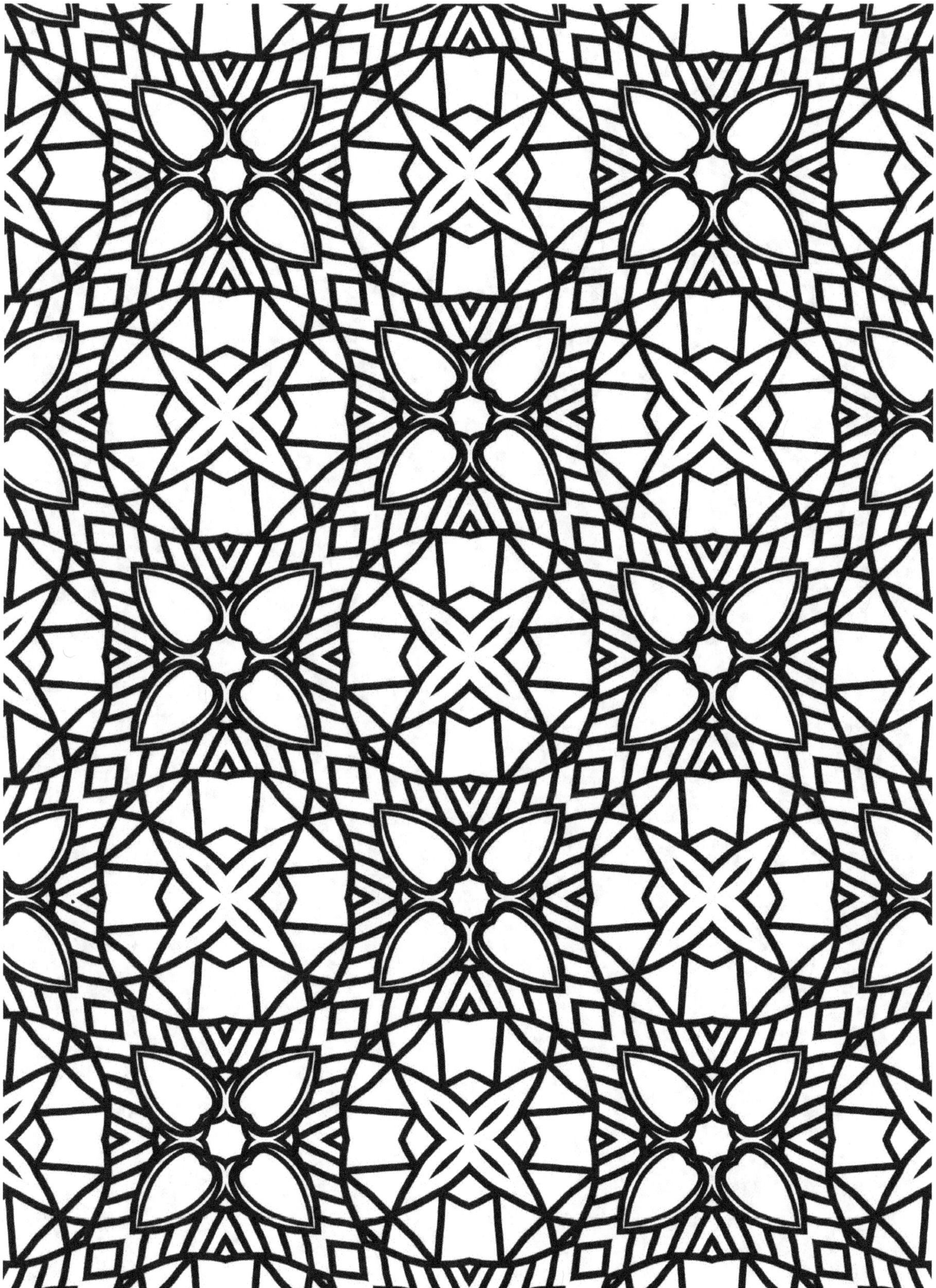

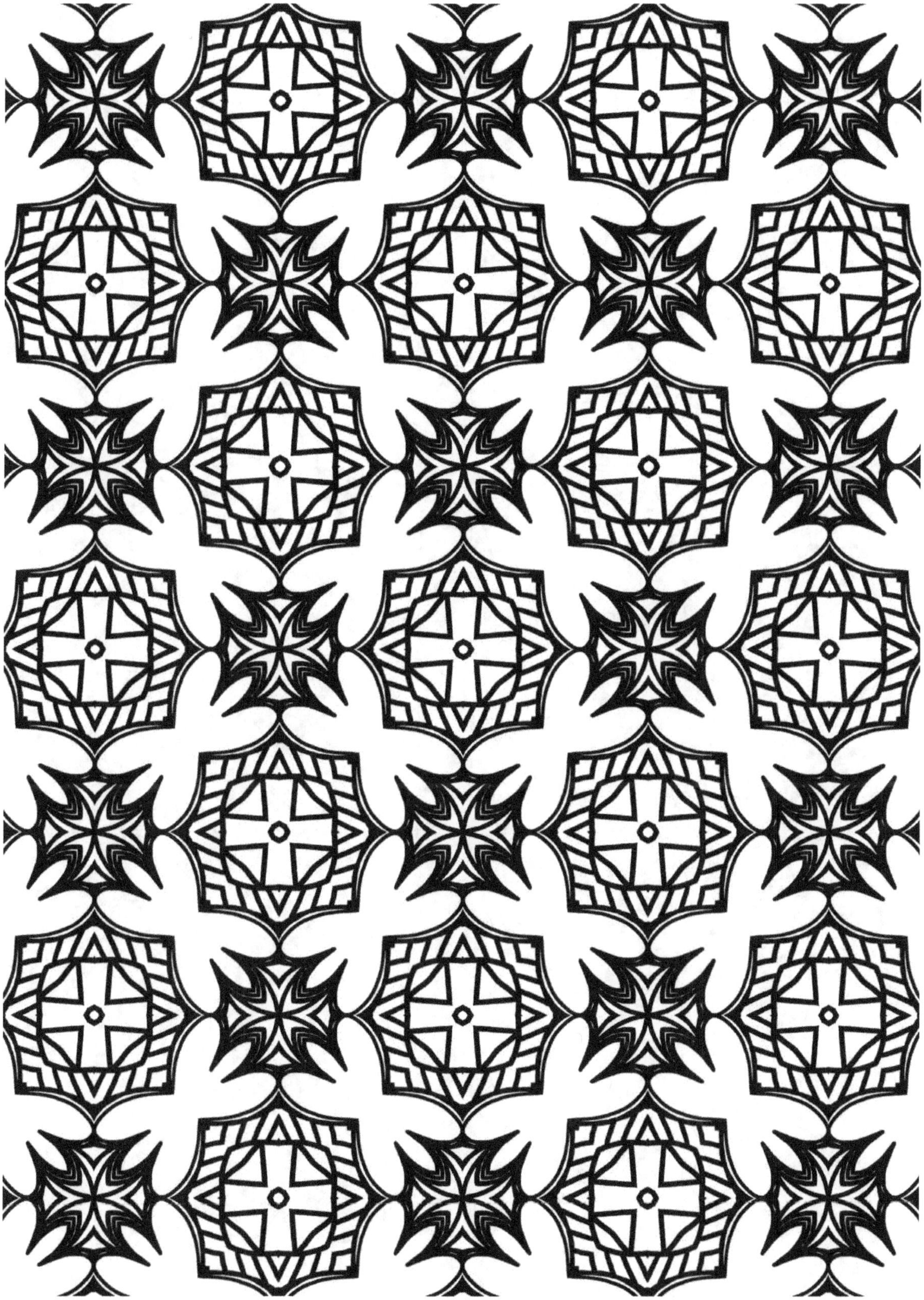

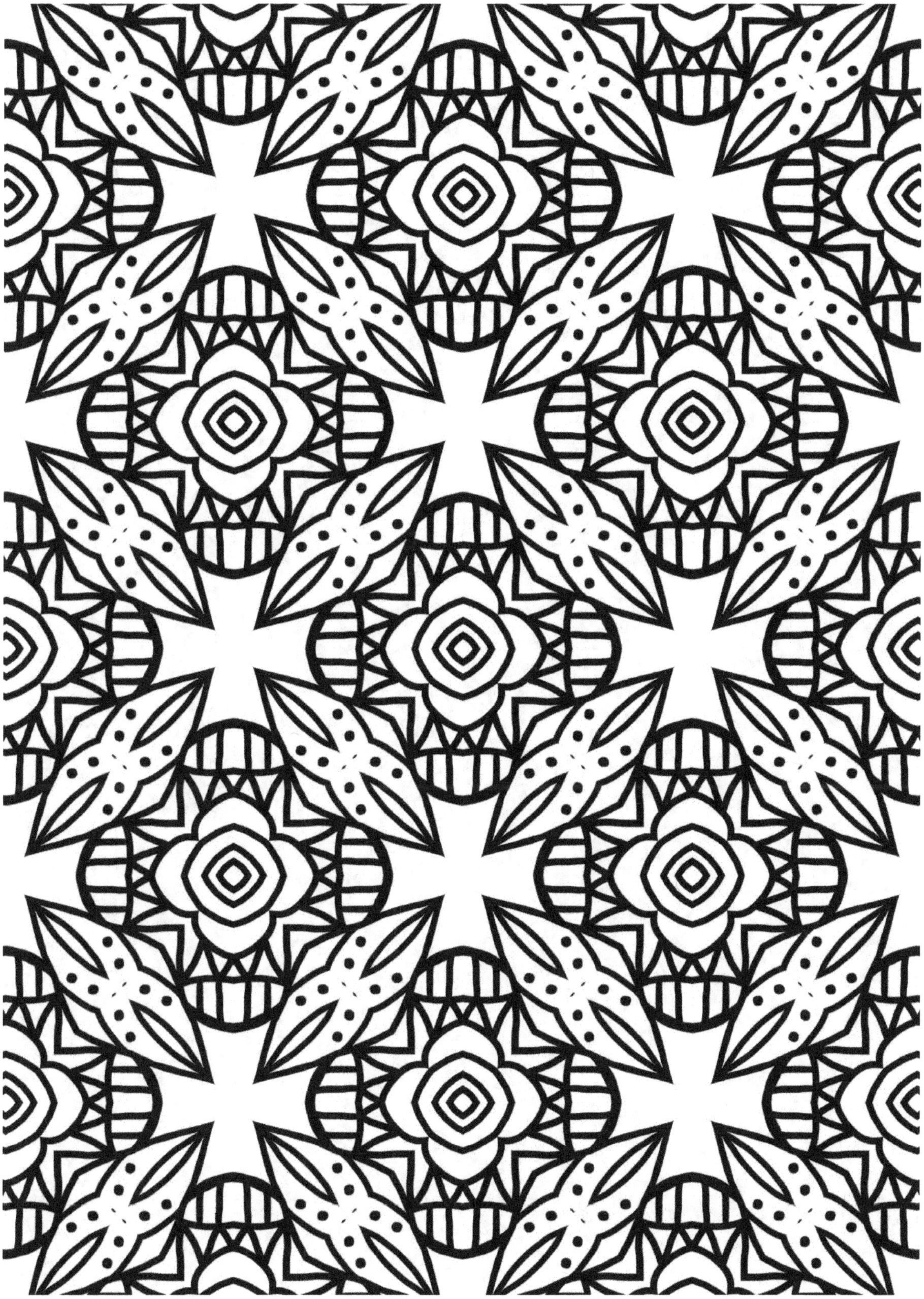

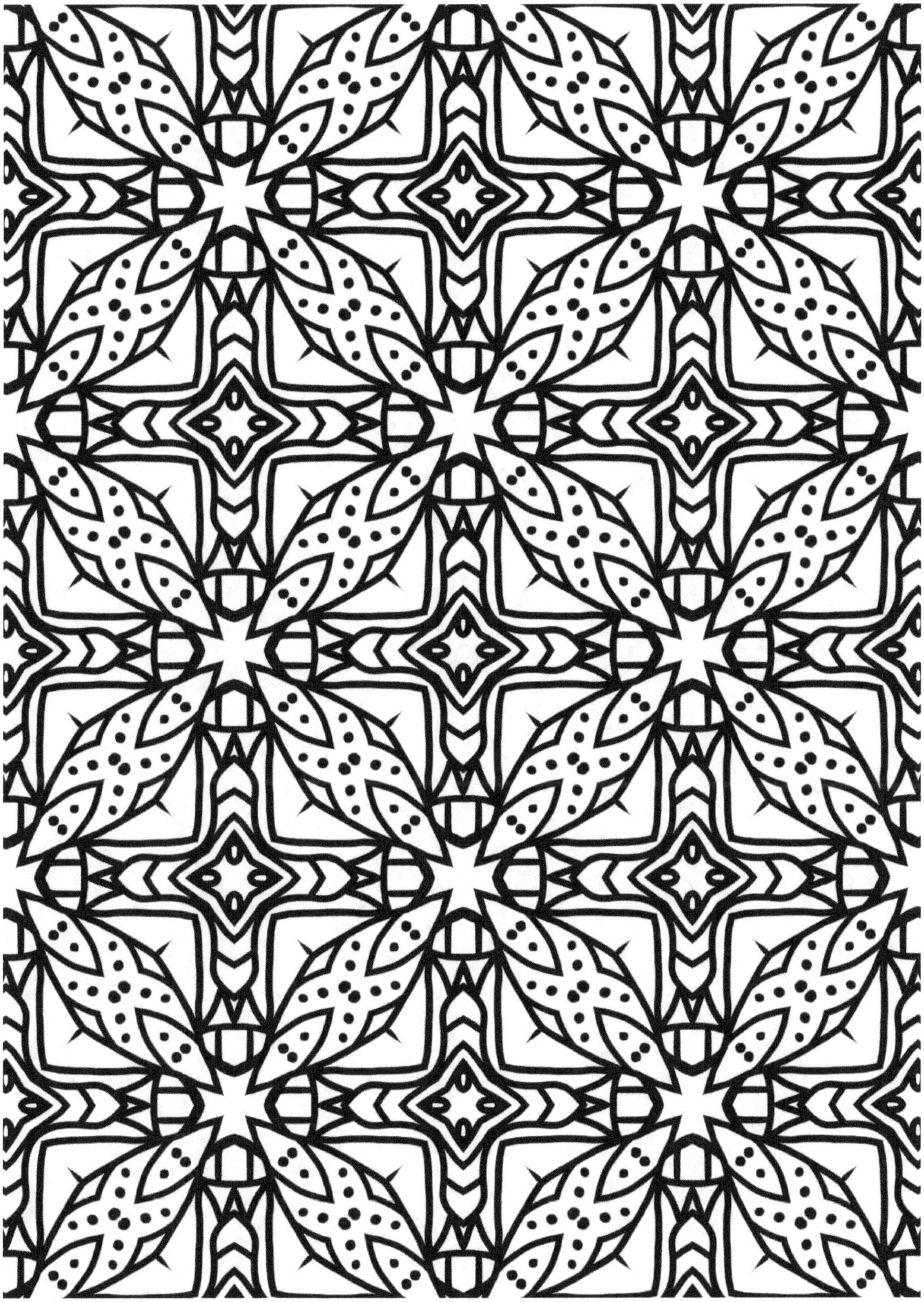

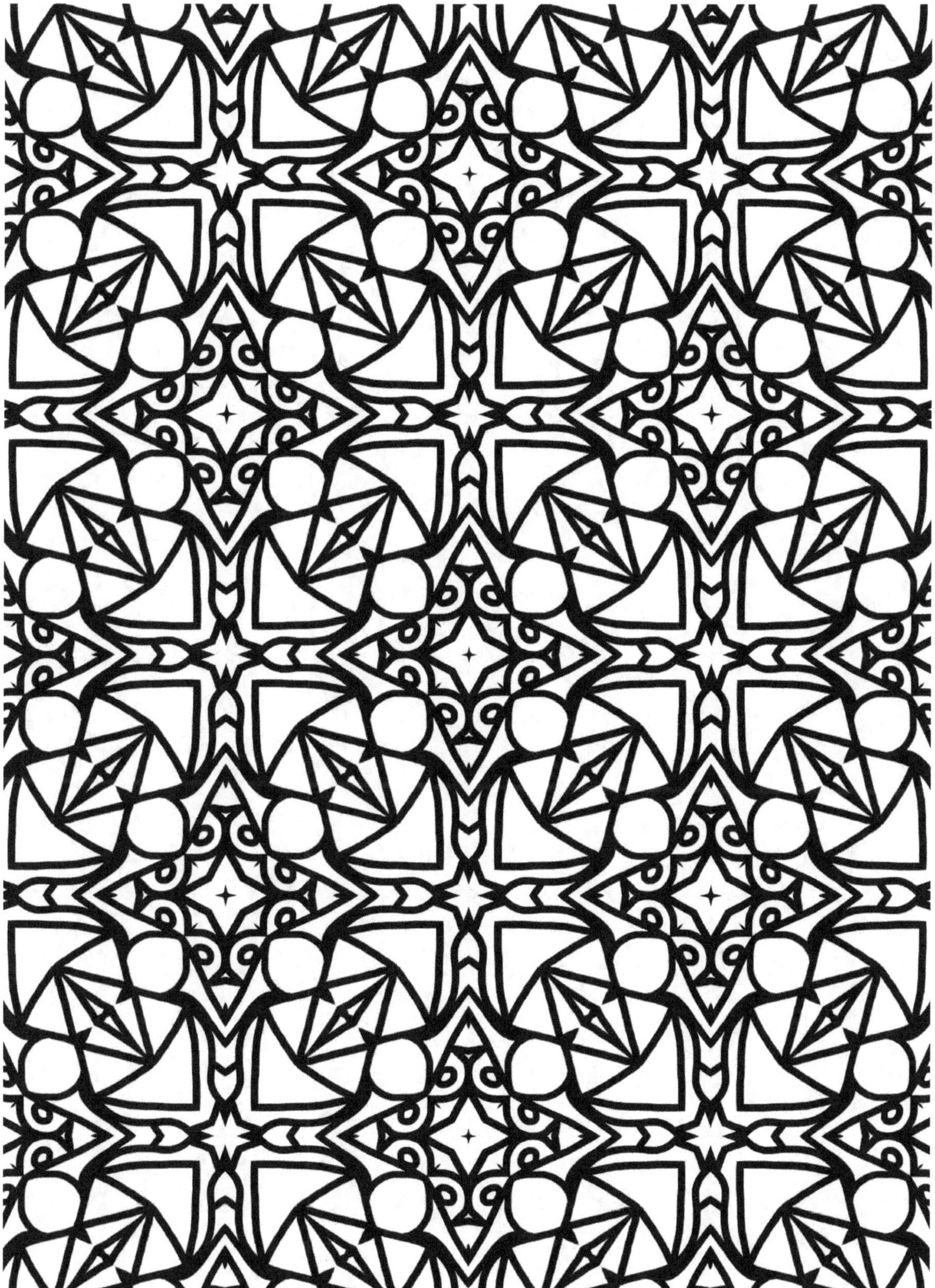

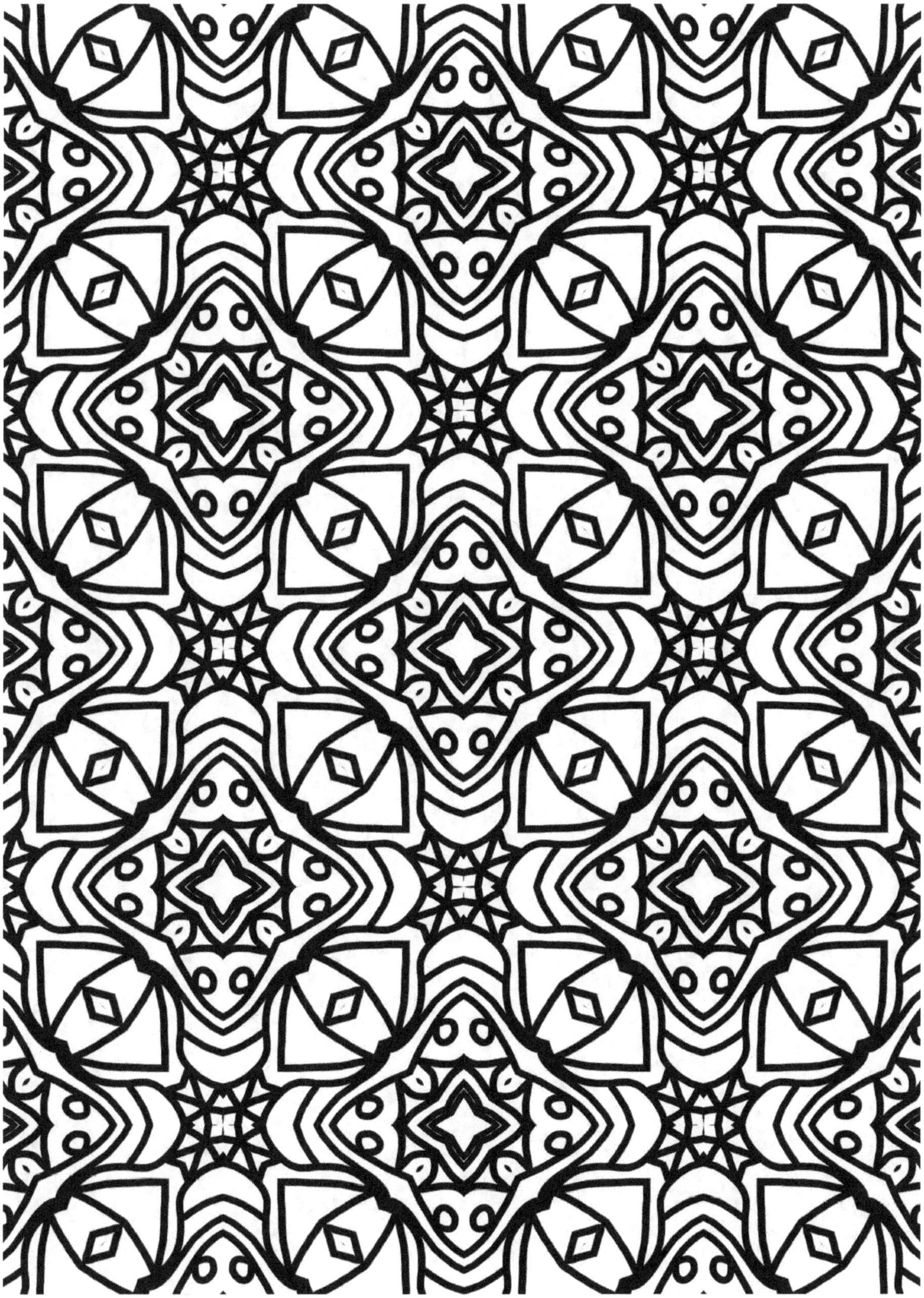

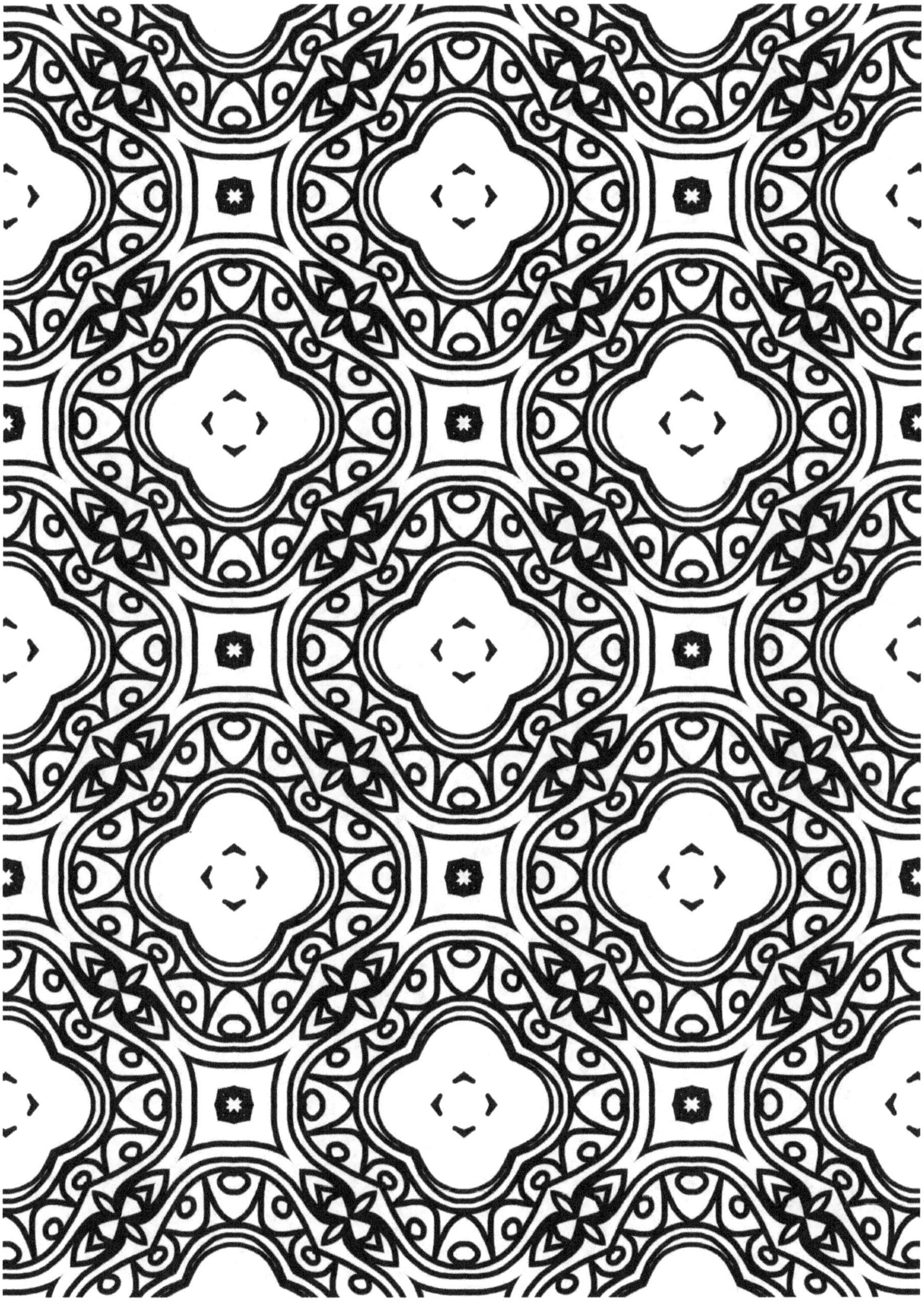

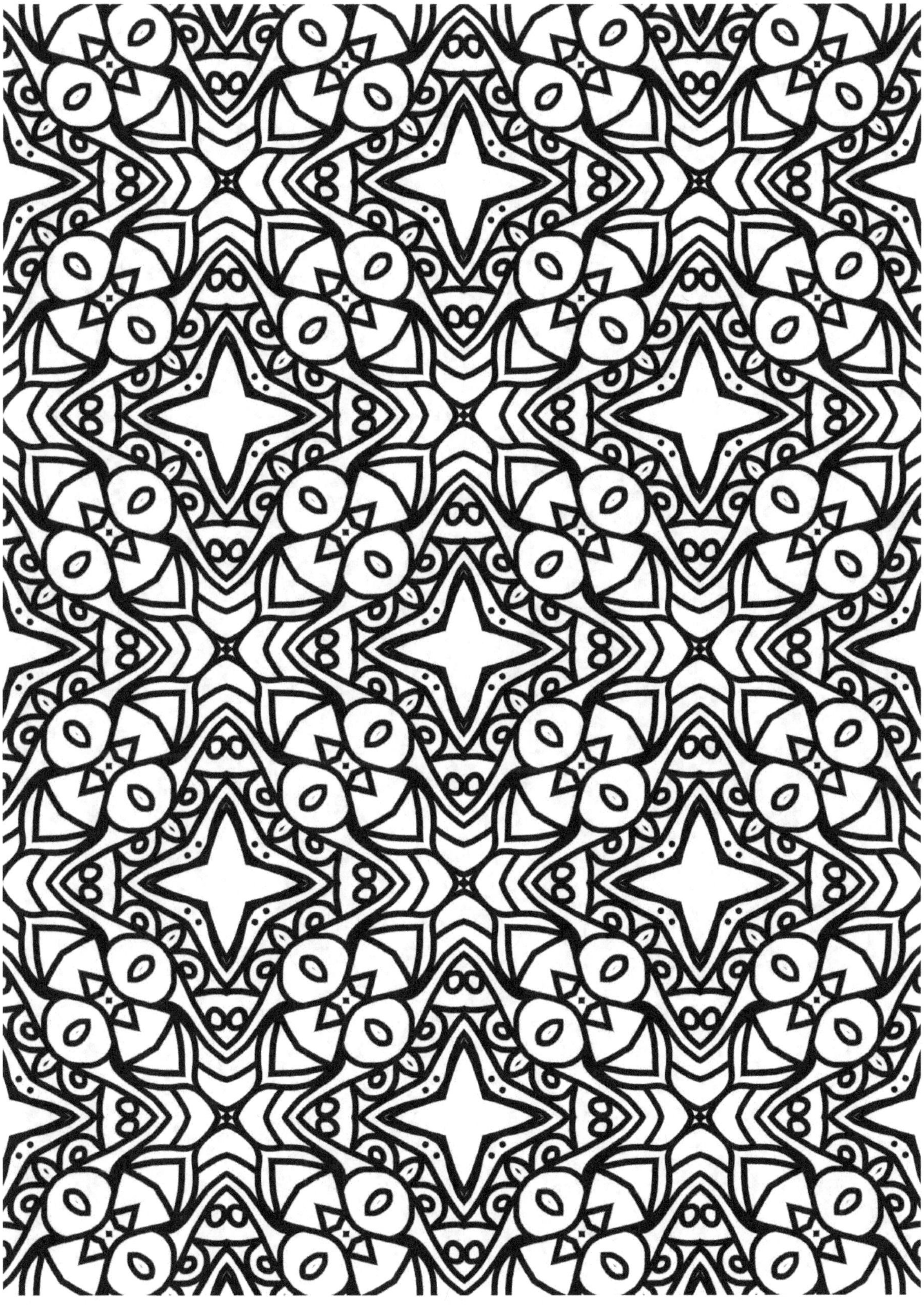

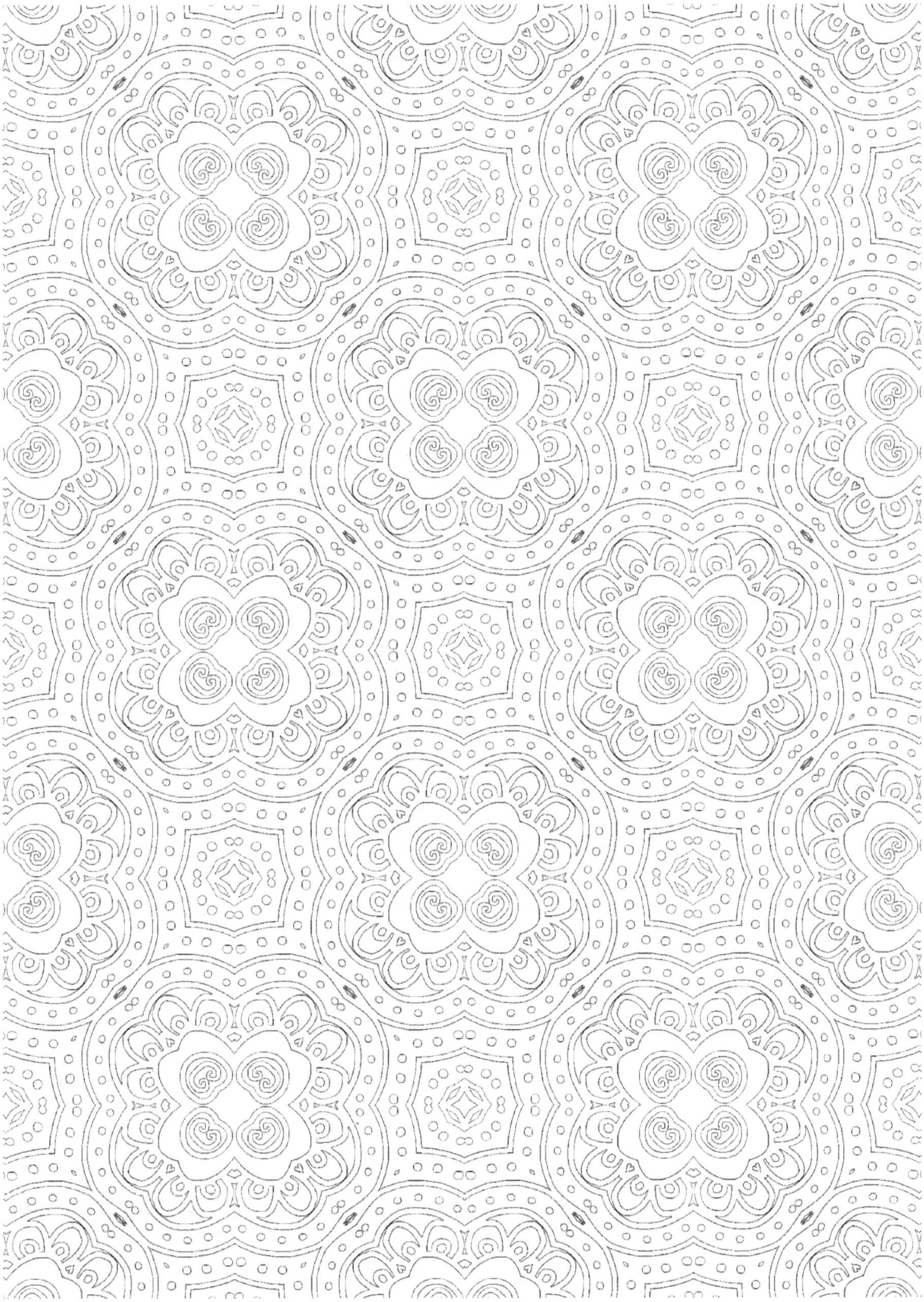

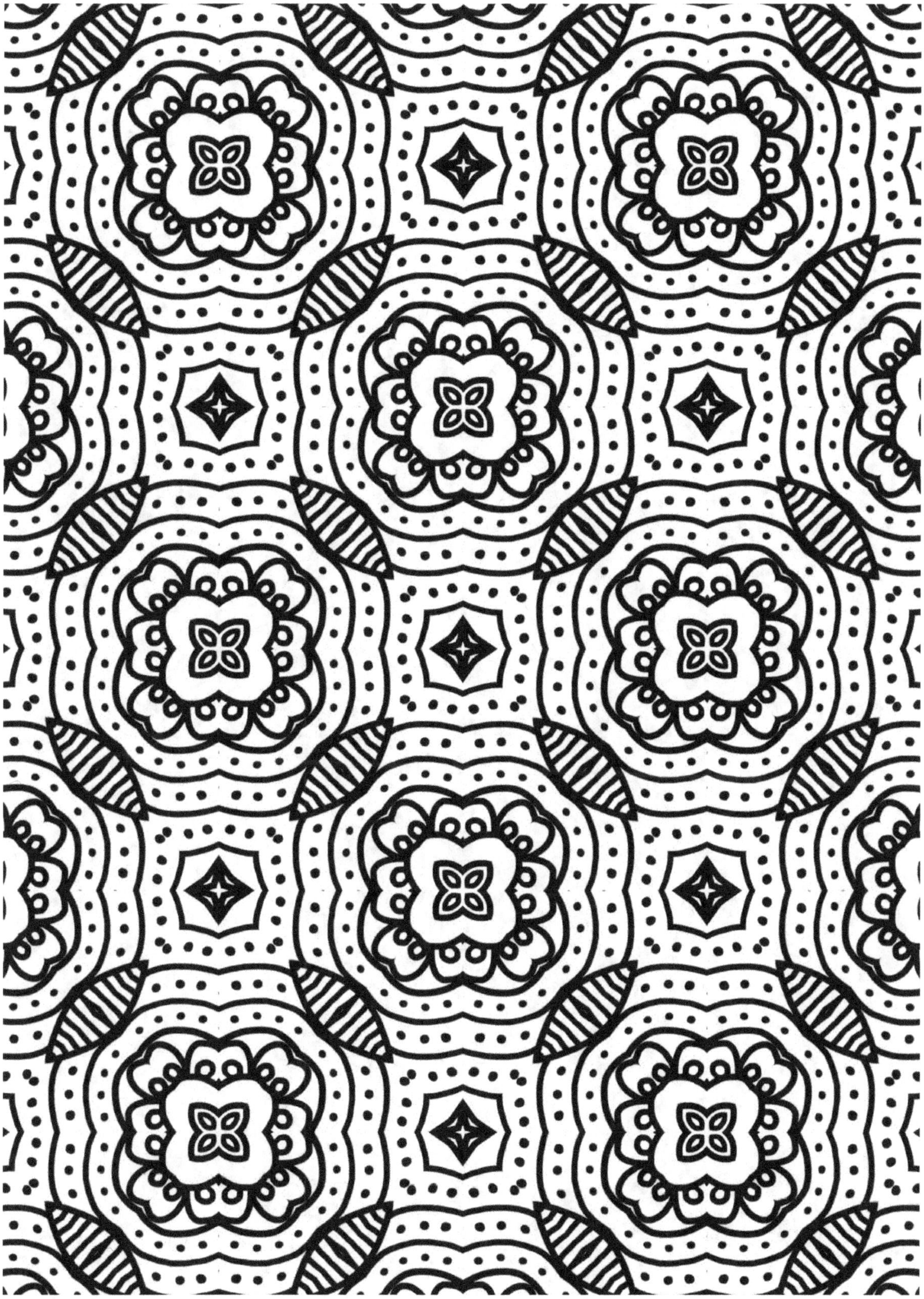

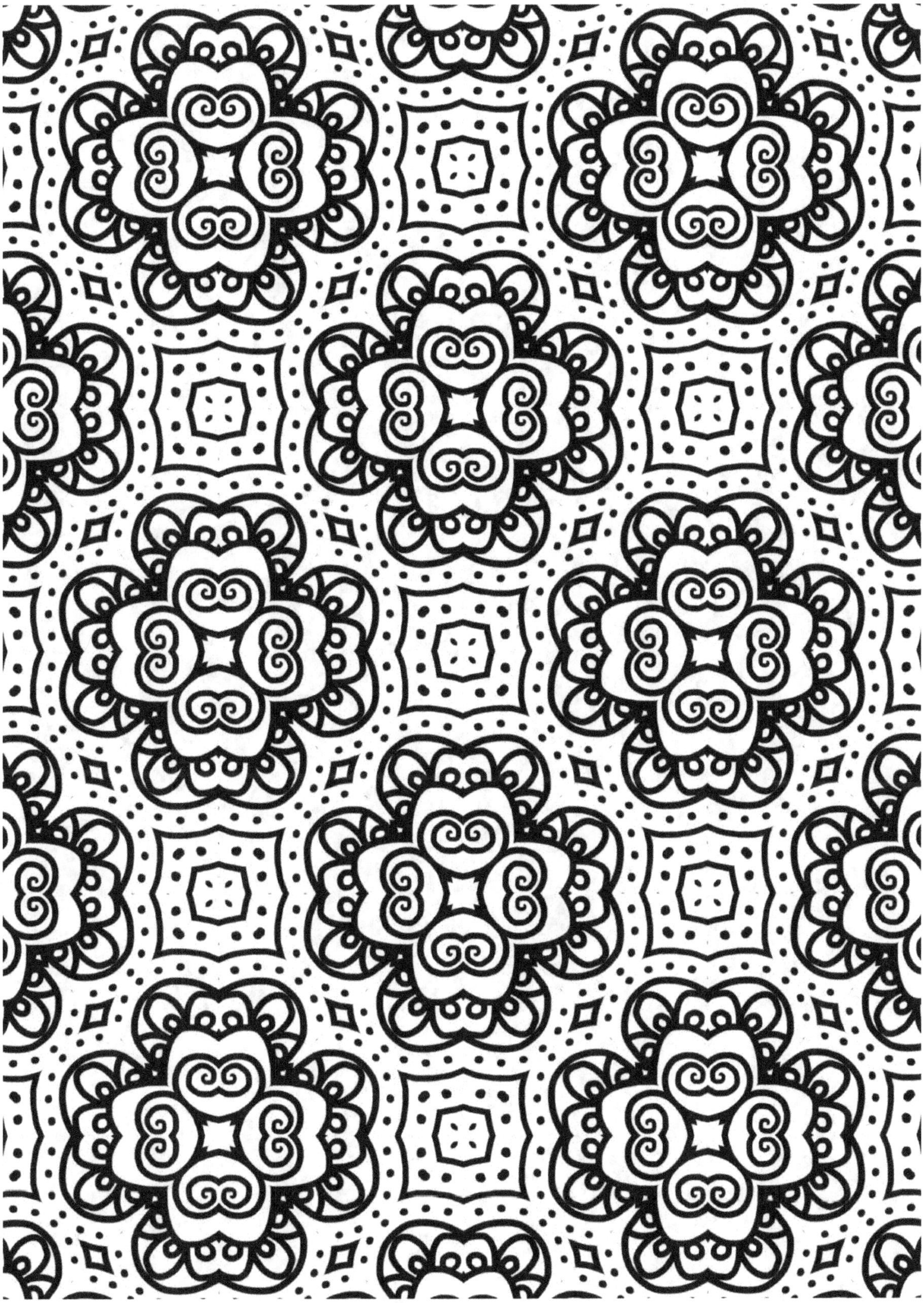

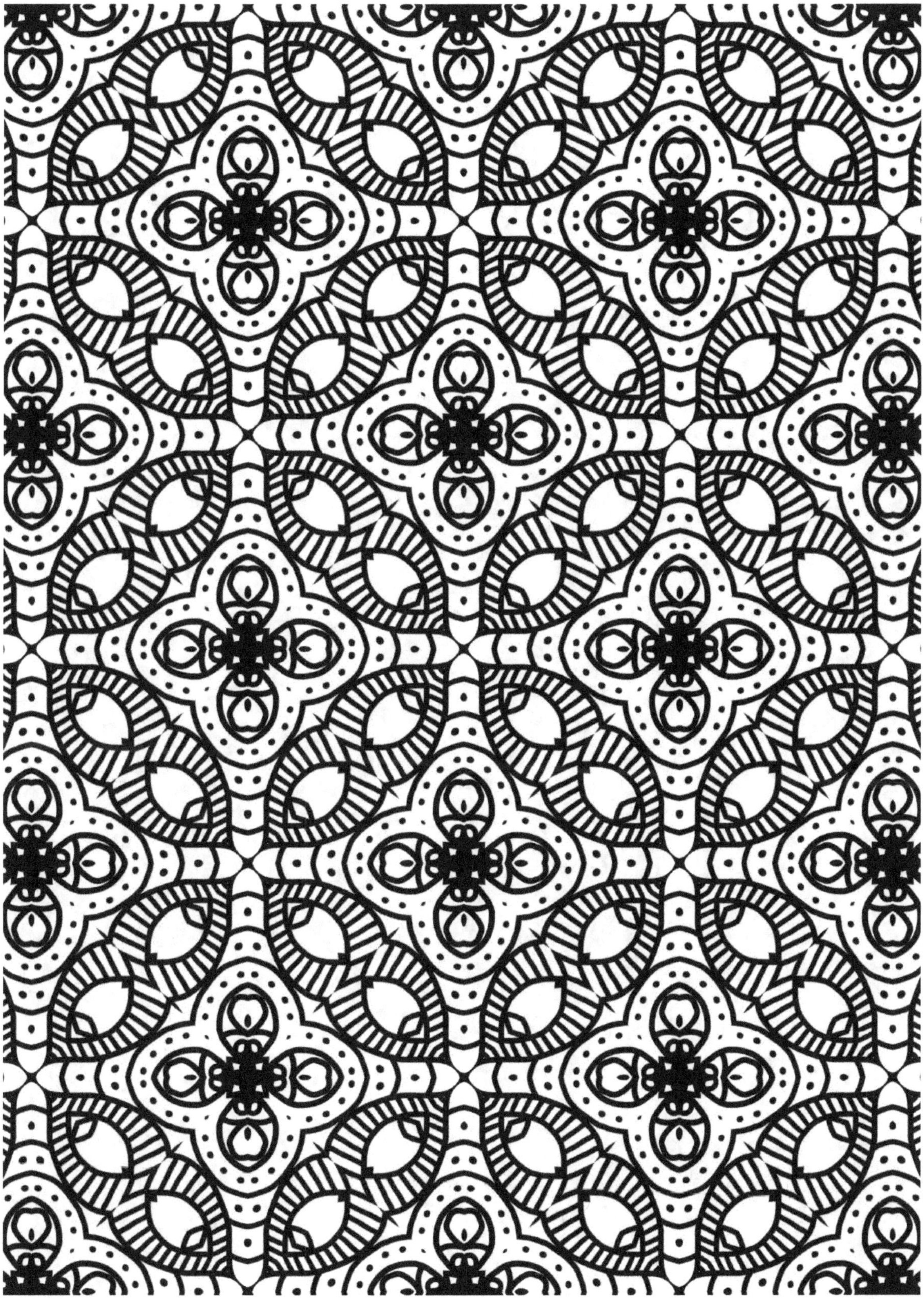

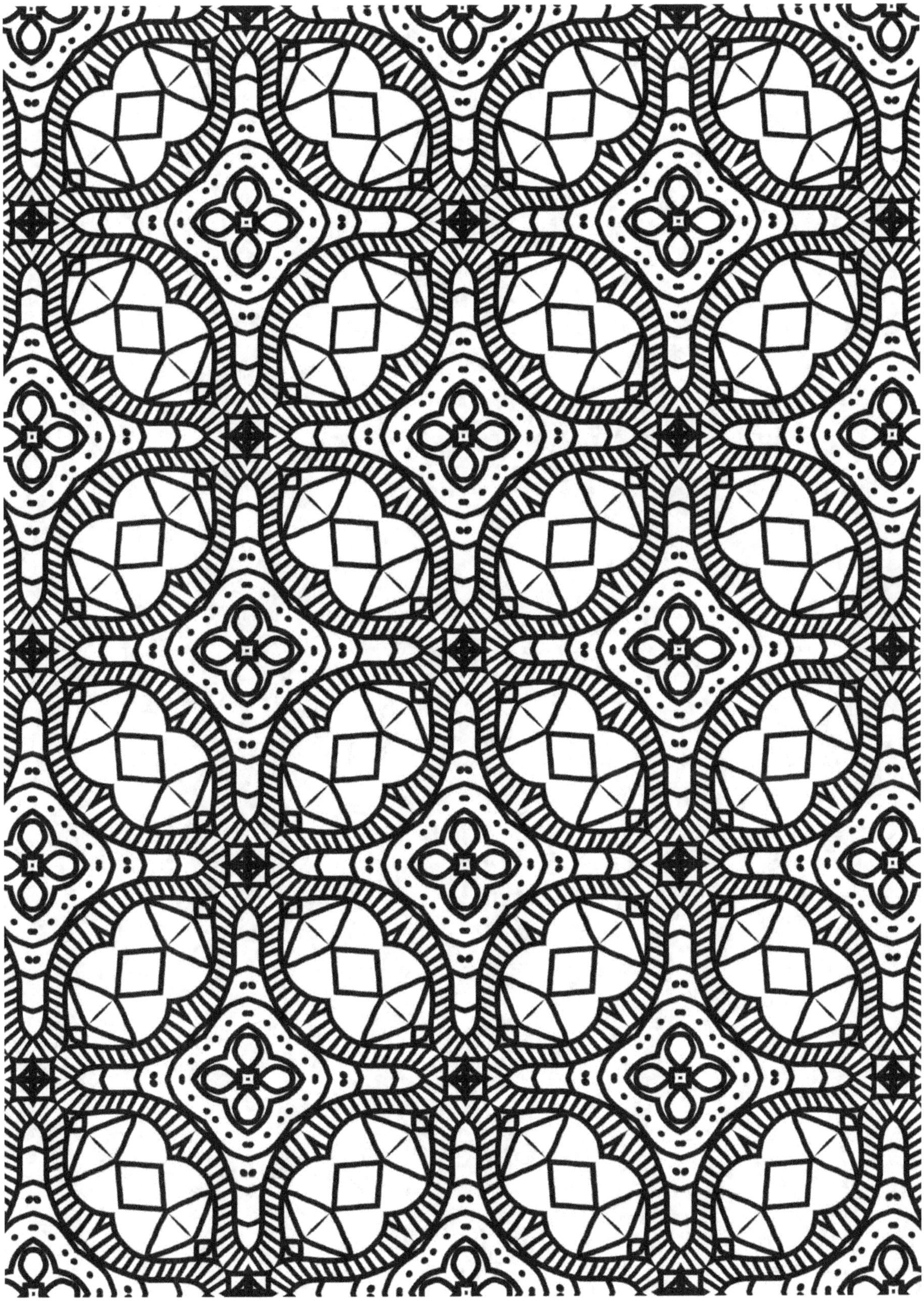

www.ingramcontent.com/pod-product-compliance
Lightning Source LLC
Chambersburg PA
CBHW081146280526
45787CB00008B/3245
* 9 7 8 1 5 3 3 4 9 4 9 7 9 *